GLENS OF

ROSS - SHIRE

THE GLENS OF
ROSS-SHIRE

A personal survey of the Glens of Ross-shire
for mountainbikers and walkers

by

Peter D. Koch - Osborne

CICERONE PRESS

MILNTHORPE, CUMBRIA, ENGLAND

© P.D. Koch-Osborne 2000
ISBN 1 85284 296 2

British Library Cataloguing-in-Publication Data.
A catalogue record for this book is
available from the British Library.

Through a clearing came the blaze of sun-
struck hills reflected in utterly calm water.
Its richness of varied colour gave it the likeness
of an ancient stained-glass window, but no
window ever glowed like that loch.
I had no more doubts about Glen Affric.
Its attributes were made manifest.
                        W.H. Murray
                        Undiscovered Scotland
                        Diadem Books

Cover Pictures:- Loch Fannich
                 Loch Damh

Index

Introduction

Access to the tracks on the following pages can rarely be regarded as an absolute right by the cyclist or walker. Almost all land is private and it is often only the good nature of the owners that allows us to travel unhindered over his land. In Scottish law the term trespass implies nuisance or damage. In practice sensible conduct removes any possibility of nuisance. Respect the grouse season (12 Aug to 10 Dec) and deer stalking (1 Jul to 20 Oct - stags and 21 Oct to 15 Feb - hinds). Your author has not once met with animosity in meeting 'keepers. Your good conduct will ensure continued access. Cyclists - stay on the trail and slow down!!

Conservation of the wild areas of Scotland is of paramount importance. Much has been written elsewhere but users of this guide must appreciate that the very ground over which you walk or cycle will be damaged if care is not taken. Please don't use a bike on soft peat paths and tread carefully on other than a stony track. Many of the tracks are in themselves an eyesore and any "development" can cause irreparable damage. Make sure, as walkers and cyclists, we encourage the conservation of our wilderness areas without the pressure of our activities causing further damage. In publishing this book a great deal of trust is placed upon you, the reader, to respect the needs of the region. If all you need is exercise - go to a sports centre! but if you appreciate the unique qualities of the wild places they are yours to enjoy..... carefully! Careless conduct not only damages what we seek to enjoy but, equally seriously, gives landowners good reason to restrict access.

<u>The Maps</u> on the following pages give sufficient detail for exploration of the glens but the Ordnance Survey Landranger maps of the region should also be used if the full geographical context of the area is to be fully appreciated. These maps and the knowledge of their proper use are essential if a long tour or cross country route is to be undertaken.

<u>The mountain bike</u>, or ATB - all terrain bike, has in the author's opinion been badly named. It does not belong on the high tops but is ideal in the glens covering at least twice the distance of the average walker, quietly, whilst still allowing a full appreciation of the surroundings and providing further exploration into the wilderness especially on short winter days. The bike must be a well maintained machine complete with a few essential spares as a broken bike miles from anywhere can be serious. Spare gear is best carried in strong panniers on good carriers. Poor quality bikes and accessories simply will not last. Front panniers help distribute weight and prevent "wheelies." Mud-guards are essential. Heavy rucksacks are tiring and put more weight onto one's already battered posterior! The brightly coloured "high profile" image of mountainbiking is unsuited to the remote glens. These wild areas are sacred and need treating as such.

<u>Clothing</u> for the mountainbiker is an important consideration, traditional road cycling gear is un-suitable. High ankle trainers are best for summer, and light weight walking boots for winter cycling. A zipped fleece jacket with waterproof top and overtrousers with spare thin sweatshirts etc

should be included for easily adjusting temperature. The wearing of a helmet is a personal choice, it depends how you ride, where you ride and the value you place on your head! In any event a thin balaclava will be required under a helmet in winter or a thick one in place of a helmet. Good waterproof gloves are essential. Fingers and ears get painfully cold on a long descent at −5°C. Protection against exposure should be as for mountain walking. Many of the glens are as high as English hilltops. The road cyclists shorts or longs will keep legs warm in summer only. In winter walker's breeches and overtrousers are more suitable.

Clothing for the walker has had much written about it elsewhere. Obviously full waterproofs, spare warm clothing, spare food etc. should be included. In winter conditions the longer through routes should never be attempted alone or by the inexperienced.

Mountainbikers and walkers alike should never be without a good map, this book (!), a whistle (and knowledge of its proper use), compass, emergency rations, and in winter a sleeping bag and cooker may be included even if an overnight stop is not planned. Word of your planned route should be left together with your estimated time of arrival. The bothies must be left tidy with firewood for the next visitor. Don't be too proud to remove someone else's litter. Join the Mountain Bothies Association to help support the maintenance of these simple shelters. It should not be necessary to repeat the Country Code and the Mountain Bike Code, the true lover of the wild places needs peace and space - not rules and regulations.

River crossings are a major consideration when planning long or "through" routes virtually anywhere in Scotland. It must be remembered that snowmelt from the high mountains can turn what is a fordable stream in early morning into a raging torrent by mid afternoon. Walkers should hold on to each other, in three's, forming a triangle if possible. Rivers can be easier to cross with a bike, as the bike can be moved, brakes applied, leant on, then the feet can be re-positioned and so on. The procedure is to remove boots and socks, replace boots, make sure you can't drop anything and cross - ouch! Drain boots well, dry your feet and hopefully your still dry socks will help to warm your feet up. Snowmelt is so cold it hurts. Choose a wide shallow point to cross and above all don't take risks.

Ascents on a bike should be tackled steadily in a very low gear and sitting down wherever possible. While front panniers prevent "wheelies" sitting down helps the rear wheel grip. Standing on the pedals causes wheel slip, erosion, and is tiring. Pushing a laden mountainbike is no fun and usually the result of tackling the lower half of a climb standing up, in the wrong gear or too fast.

Descents on a bike can be exhilarating but a fast descent is hard on the bike, the rider, and erodes the track if wheels are locked. It is also ill-mannered towards others who may be just around the next bend.

Last but not least other users of the tracks need treating with respect - it may be the owner! Bad conduct can only lead to restricted access, spoiling it for us all.

The Maps 1

The maps are drawn to depict the most important features to the explorer of the glens. North is always at the top of each map and all maps, apart from the detail sketches, are to the same scale :- 1km or 0·6 miles being shown on each map. An attempt has been made to present the maps in a pictorially interesting way. A brief explanation of the various features is set out below :-

<u>Tracks</u> :- One of the prime objects of this book is to grade the tracks according to "roughness". This information is essential to the mountainbiker and useful to the walker. With due respect to the Ordnance Survey one "other road, drive or track" can take twice as long to cycle along as another yet both may be depicted in the same way. The author's attempt at grading is set out below :-

metalled road, not too many fortunately, public roads are generally included only to locate the start of a route.

good track, hardly rutted, nearly as fast as a road to cycle on but can be boring to walk far on.   Most are forest tracks.

the usual rutted "Landrover" track, rough but all easily rideable on a mountainbike, not too tedious to walk on.

rough, very rutted track nearly all rideable, can be very rough even for walking. Either very stony or overgrown or boggy.

walker's path, usually over 50% is rideable and included especially as a part of a through route. Details given on each map.

<u>Relief</u> is depicted in two ways. The heavy black lines are now a commonly used method of depicting main mountain summits, ridges and spurs thus :-

Contour lines are also used, at 50m intervals up to about 600m. This adds "shape" to the glens as mapped and gives the reader an idea of how much climbing is involved. Reference to the gradient profiles at the start of each section compares the various routes :-

<u>Crags</u> in the high mountains are shown thus :-

....with major areas of scree shown dotted

<u>Rivers</u> generally "uncrossable" are shown as two lines whilst streams, generally "crossable" are shown using a single line. Note :- great care is needed crossing even the larger streams. Falling in can cause embarrassment at best, exposure or drowning at worst. Please don't take risks - besides you'd get this book wet !!

loch or lochan

<u>Buildings</u> and significant ruins are shown as a :- ■

<u>Bridges</u> are rather obviously shown thus :-

There are so many trees I wish there were an easier way of drawing them - but there isn't ! I'm fed up with drawing trees !!

etc etc.....

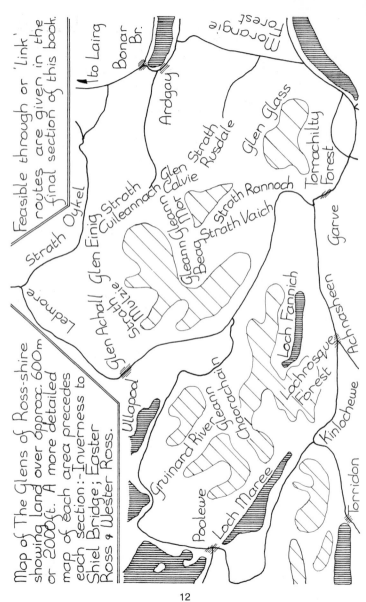

Map of The Glens of Ross-shire showing land over approx. 600m or 2000ft. A more detailed map of each area precedes each section:- Inverness to Shiel Bridge; Easter Ross & Wester Ross.

Feasible through or 'Link' routes are given in the final section of this book.

to Lairg

Bonar Br.

Morangie Forest

Ardgay

Glen Glass

Torrachilty Forest

Strath Oykel

Strath Cuileannach

Glen Einig

Glen Strath Calvie Rusdale

Strath Rannoch

Garve

Ledmore

Glen Achall

Strath Mulzie

Gleann Mor Gleann Beag Strath Vaich

Strath Vaich

Achnasheen

Ullapool

Gruinard River

Gleann Chaorachain

Loch Fannich

Lochrosque Forest

Poolewe

Loch Maree

Kinlochewe

Torridon

12

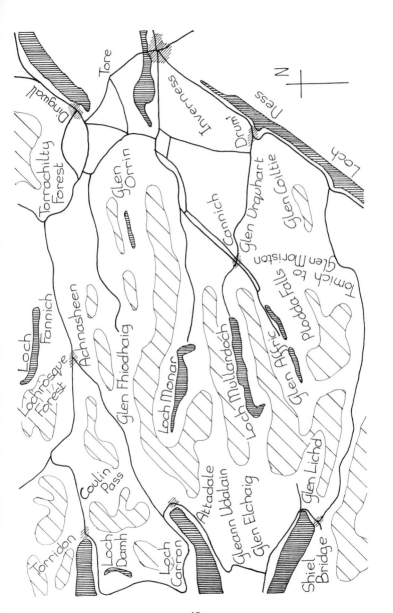

Dingwall

Tore

Inverness

Drum'

Loch Ness

Torrachilty Forest

Glen Orrin

Cannich

Glen Urquhart

Glen Coiltie

Tomich to Glen Moriston

Plodda Falls

Glen Affric

Loch Fannich

Achnasheen

Glen Fhiodhaig

Loch Monar

Loch Mullardoch

Lochrosque Forest

Coulin Pass

Attadale

Gleann Udalain

Glen Elchaig

Glen Lichd

Torridon

Loch Damh

Loch Carron

Shiel Bridge

N

Inverness to Shiel Bridge

Inverness to Shiel Bridge

Access:- This region encompasses the southern extremities of this guide from west to east, bordered by the A87 Glen Shiel, A887 Glen Moriston and A82 Great Glen roads. Access is therefore easy from either the west (via Fort William and Loch Lochy) or from Inverness and the A9.

Accommodation:- Inverness has everything as has Drumnadrochit though in lesser quantity. Both the above do get very busy. West of these centres the two SYHA hostels at Loch Ness and especially Ratagan both provide a good base. Cannich hostel is very well placed for Affric and Plodda. Cluanie Inn is an hotel; b&b's thin out (indeed so does any habitation!) as one heads west, until Shiel Bridge is reached.

Geographical Features:- Almost the entire area is wild. Forest and moorland to the east, further west the glens narrow between shapely peaks. Glen Shiel is squeezed in between the Five Sisters Ridge and the South Kintail Ridge providing a dramatic approach to Shiel Bridge from the east. It is worth noting just how far west the east/west watersheds are.

Mountains:- The Five Sisters of Kintail, best viewed from near Ratagan Youth Hostel, are deservedly well known, with the South Kintail Ridge a close second place. A cluster of 3000 footers lies north and east of the Five Sisters and many of the tracks described can be used (by bike) to assist access to these fine hills. Further east the tops are rounded moors but exceptionally wild despite only just beating the 2000ft contour.

Rivers:- Most of the region drains to the east and these rivers suffer the usual Scottish characteristic of changing their name as they progress. The River Affric drains the north of the region, becoming the River Glass before changing its identity once again to the River Beauly on the final 'leg' to the Beauly Firth. The River Moriston flows out of Cluanie dam, having set out as the River Cluanie, on its way to Loch Ness. The River Coiltie also flows to Loch Ness down a glen of the same name, whilst the River Enrick drains Glen Urquhart. In the west the River Shiel makes its short dash for the sea and the even shorter River Croe drains Glen Lichd. There are no difficult river crossings unless spate conditions prevail.

Forests:- The main areas are Glen Affric, Plodda Falls and Glen Urquhart. Glen Affric is the best as it includes Scots Pine (your author's favourite tree), and thanks to planting these forests spill over to Plodda Falls and their combined access roads provide much good cycling. Glen Urquhart's forests are not as interesting but a good network of tracks lies alongside this peaceful glen, again giving good biking.

Lochs:- Loch Ness, complete with alleged monster, borders the region as does the dammed Loch Cluanie. Loch Beinn a Mheadhoin and Loch Affric are the most picturesque. A scattering of remote fishing lochans occupy the remote eastern moors. Loch Duich and the Beauly Firth flank the region, both linked by narrows to the open sea.

Emergency:- All routes start from populated areas but soon run out into wild country. Affric hostel is only open in summer but provides a haven. Always remember to let someone know where you are going – and report back.

Inverness to Shiel Bridge Routes 1

Glen Coiltie

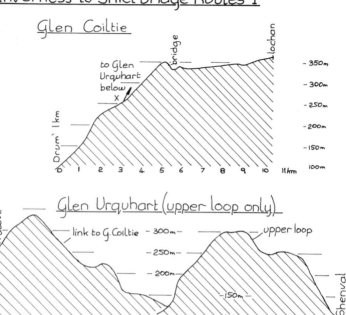

Glen Urquhart (upper loop only)

Tomich to Glen Moriston

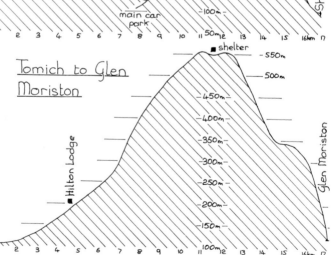

Plodda Falls

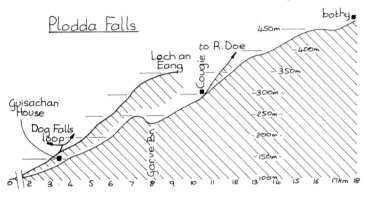

Glen Affric

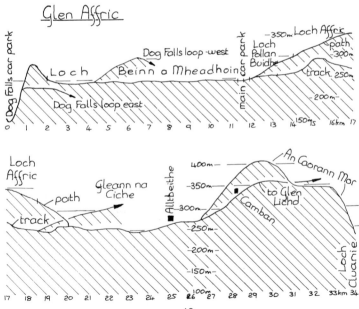

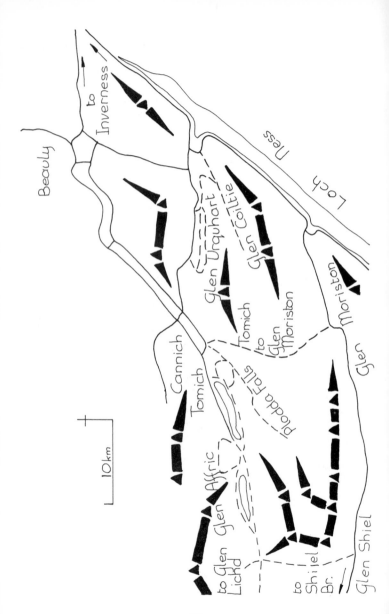

Beauly

to Inverness

Loch Ness

Glen Urquhart

Glen Coiltie

Glen Moriston

Tomich to Glen Moriston

Glen Moriston

Glen

Cannich

Tomich

Dog Fall Plodda Falls

10 km

Glen Affric

Glen Lichd

to Glen Lichd

to Shiel Br.

Glen Shiel

Glen Shiel

Glen Coiltie 1

Once out of the woods the Glen Coiltie track becomes rough and progress on a bike is slow to the strange house-on-the-island at Loch Aslaich. The first couple of miles of track provide a connection between Drumnadrochit and the many tracks contouring above Glen Urquhart – see the next route. The distance to Loch Aslaich from the start of the track is 11 km or 7 miles (add 2km or 1·5 miles from downtown Drum'.) There is no shelter in Glen Coiltie.

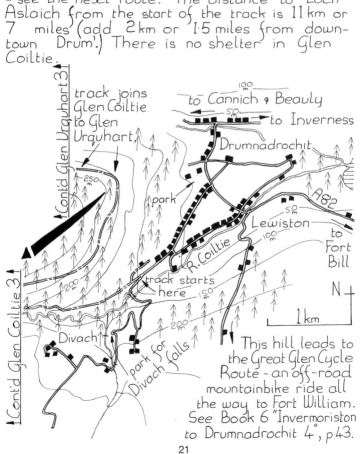

Cont'd Glen Urquhart 3

track joins Glen Coiltie to Glen Urquhart.

100 m

to Cannich & Beauly

50

to Inverness

Drumnadrochit

250 m

park

A82

50 m

Lewiston

100 m

to Fort Bill

R. Coiltie

200 m

track starts here

150

N

1 km

Cont'd Glen Coiltie 3

Divach

park for Divach falls

200

This hill leads to the Great Glen Cycle Route - an off-road mountainbike ride all the way to Fort William. See Book 6 "Invermoriston to Drumnadrochit 4", p 43.

21

Glen Coiltie 2

Only a few short miles from Drum', the Glen Coiltie track feels as remote as any – it touches on an almost completely unfrequented area of small fishing lochs.

A rough landscape of hill, rock outcrop and heather moor; and best of all, almost total solitude.

481m

Carn an t- Sluic Dhuibh 567m

450 m

400 m

350 m

400 m

N

1km

ford

River Coiltie

Strathan Allt na Fiacail

450 m

Loch Aslaich

Continued opposite

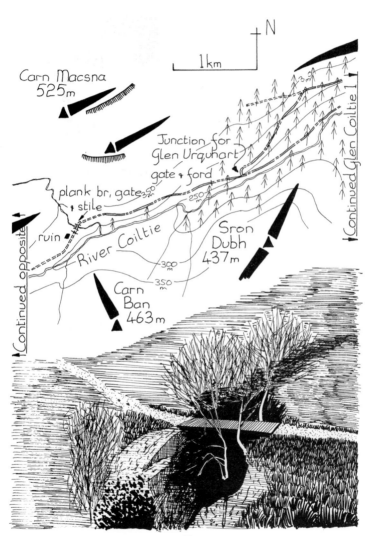

N

1km

Carn Macsna
525m

Junction for
Glen Urquhart

gate & ford

plank br, gate
& stile

350 m

250 m

ruin

River Coiltie

Sron
Dubh
437m

300 m

350 m

Carn
Ban
463m

◄ Continued opposite

Continued Glen Coiltie 1 ►

Glen Urquhart 1

The forest tracks above Glen Urquhart provide an endless, but not uninteresting, variety of routes for mountainbiking; contouring at various levels above the glen. Access is from the main car park with road connections at 'X'-the start of the Corrimony road; 'Y' Shenval; and 'Z' Shewglie. A further link connects Glen Urquhart with Glen Coiltie, the lower section of the latter track being good in contrast with its rough upper reaches. Distance is to choice, either a half day or a full day may be spent exploring these tracks. However a full day is required if the head of Glen Coiltie is to be included. There is no shelter other than the bus shelter at Shenval. Note the picnic table (below) at the western end of the forest.

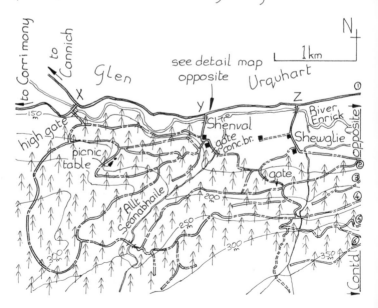

Glen Urquhart 2

The environs of Shenval

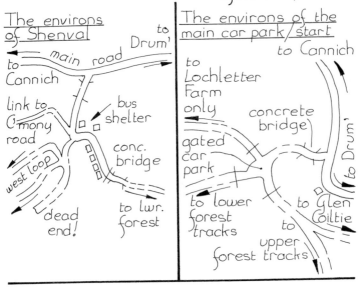

to Drum'

main road

to Cannich

link to 'mony road

bus shelter

conc. bridge

west loop

dead end!

to lwr. forest

The environs of the main car park/start

to Cannich

to Lochletter Farm only

concrete bridge

gated car park

to lower forest tracks

to Glen Coiltie

to upper forest tracks

to Drum'

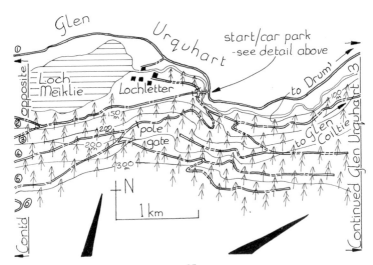

Glen Urquhart

start/car park -see detail above

Loch Meiklie

Lochletter

to Drum'

opposite

150 m

200

200

pole gate

300 m

to Glen Coiltie

N

1 km

Continued Glen Urquhart 3

Contid

Glen Urquhart 3

Forestry - above
Loch Ness

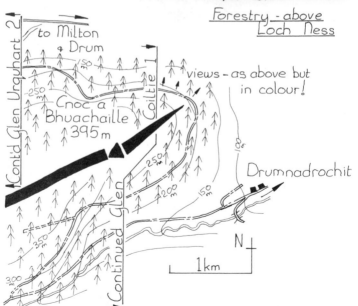

to Milton
& Drum

150

Contd Glen Urquhart 2

250
m

Cnoc a
Bhuachaille
395 m

Coiltie 1

views - as above but
in colour!

100m

Drumnadrochit

250

200

150

Continued Glen

350

300

N

1km

The track from Tomich to Glen Moriston has many
similarities with the Corrieyairack Pass (Book 6).
It is part of the same military road; it crosses
a high pass; and unfortunately it is marred by
the same line of pylons as its better known twin.
The one-way distance is some 17km or 11miles,
and transport is needed at both ends of the
route for a complete traverse. There is
shelter near the summit of the pass in a
miserable concrete hut. The summit
lies at 560m so don't
underestimate the
amount of
climbing
required!

Dog Falls loop

Continued Glen Affric 8

to Cannich

Knockfin Br.

Tomich

Guisachan

Loch na Beinne Moire

gate

gates

gate

Continued Plodda Falls 4

gates

Guisachan Ho.

Guisachan (ruin)

conc.

monument

path to Corrimony

403m△ monument

Loch a Ghreidlein

gate

rough/overgrown

N

gate

1km

ends in 500mts.

Hilton Lodge

△ 409m

X   gate   Y

Tomich to Glen Moriston 2

Continued Tomich to Glen Moriston 1
X
Y
250 m
ruin
fords
high gate
ford
300 m
350 m
400 m
450 m
500 m
The hut
N
1 km
Loch na Beinne Baine
Carn nan Earb 663m
600 m
550 m
350
hut/ shelter
collapsed bridge
Carn Mhic an Toisich 680m
600 m
500 m
450 m
Beinn Bhan
An Suidhe
550 m
560m approx.
Continued opposite

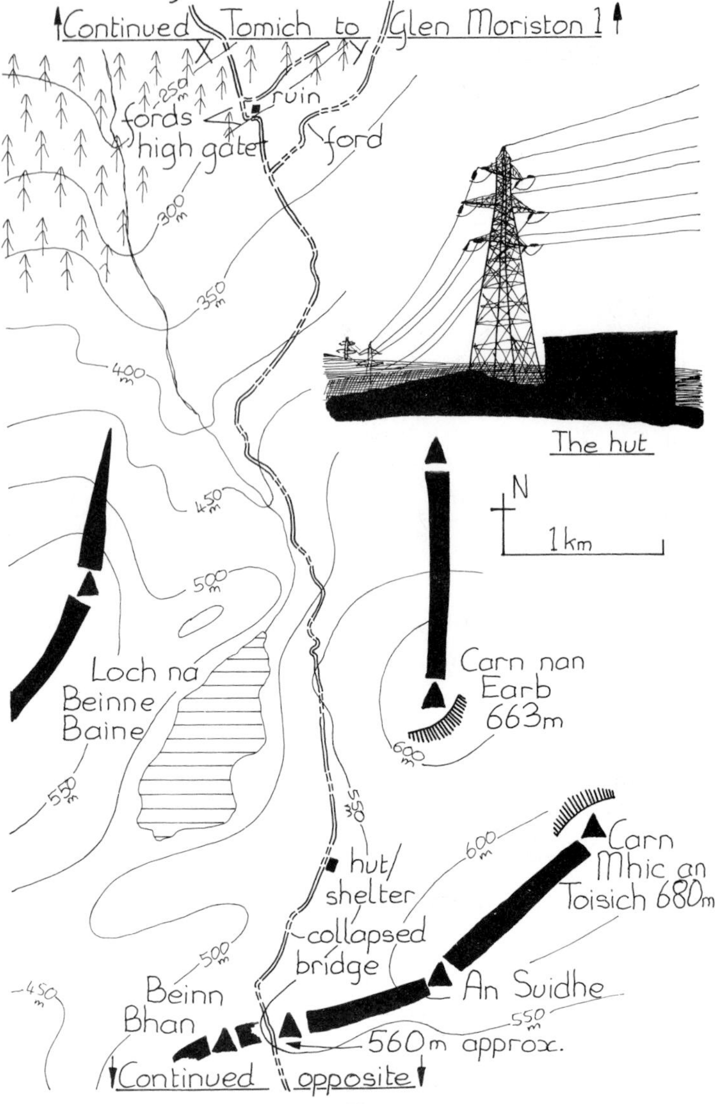

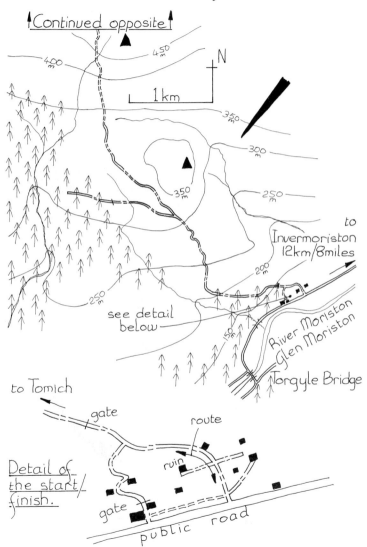

Continued opposite

N

1 km

400 m

450 m

350 m

300 m

350 m

250 m

200 m

to Invermoriston
12km/8miles

250 m

see detail
below

150 m

River Moriston
Glen Moriston

Torgyle Bridge

to Tomich

gate

route

ruin

Detail of
the start/
finish.

gate

public road

29

Plodda Falls 1

The paths and tracks around Plodda Falls provide a superb area for walker and mountainbiker alike. Cyclists may prefer to start from Tomich or even Cannich, whilst walkers are better placed starting from the Plodda Falls car park, some 5km or 3 miles beyond Tomich. (Cyclists must watch for cars on this section). The tracks may be pursued to the old bothy, below, or via the hill path above Cougie to Glen Doe. Connections to Glen Affric are: a) via either 'Leg' of the Dog Falls Loop, or b) via the very rough path (no bikes!) opposite – note this involves crossing the Allt Garbh – not advisable if in spate. The less adventurous can enjoy just pottering around the Falls and the tracks around Tomich – with its further connection to Glen Moriston, see previous section. Approximate distances are given opposite. There is shelter in the boat-house at Loch nan Gillean.

Note!
No cycling on the paths in the immediate vicinity of Plodda Falls please!!

bothy

Loch an Squid

N

1 km

873 m

Continued

opposite

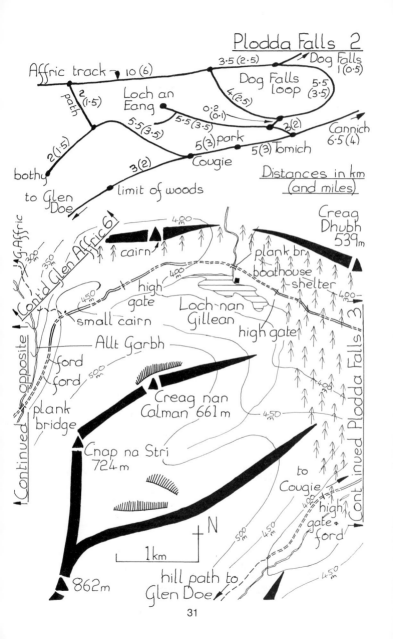

Plodda Falls 2

Affric track → 10 (6)

3·5 (2·5)

Dog Falls 1 (0·5)

Dog Falls Loop

4 (2·5)

5·5 (3·5)

2 (1·5)

path

Loch an Eang

0·2 (0·1)

5·5 (3·5)

5·5 (3·5)

2 (2)

Cannich 6·5 (4)

2 (1·5)

5 (3) park

5 (3) Tomich

bothy

Cougie

3 (2)

to Glen Doe

limit of woods

Distances in km (and miles)

Cont'd Glen Affric 6

↑ G. Affric

400 m

cairn

Creag Dhubh 539 m

plank br.

boathouse

shelter

high gate

400 m

small cairn

Loch nan Gillean

high gate

Allt Garbh

ford

ford

500 m

400 m

plank bridge

Creag nan Calman 661 m

450 m

Cnap na Stri 724 m

to Cougie

high gate

ford

↑ Continued opposite

Continued Plodda Falls 3

N

1 km

862 m

500 m

450 m

hill path to Glen Doe

450 m

31

Plodda Falls 3

The track to Loch an Eang is worth pursuing for the viewpoint. The track ends at a high gate at which point take the boggy 'path' north west for 50 metres or so.

This point is only a few hundred metres from the Affric tracks. The path north from Loch an Eang, shown on the O.S. map, is non-existent or overgrown.

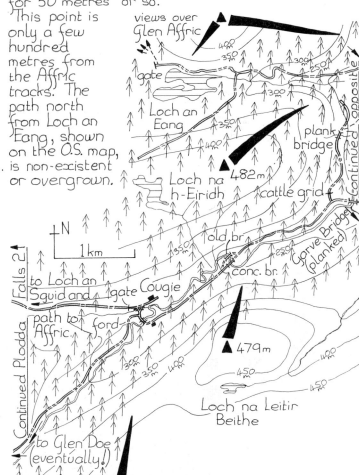

views over Glen Affric

gate

Loch an Eang

400

350

300

250

300

plank bridge

Continued opposite

482m

Loch na h-Eiridh

cattle grid

Garve Bridge (planked)

N

1 km

old br.

350

250

conc. br.

to Loch an Sguid and gate Cougie

path to Affric.

ford

300

350

400

479m

450

450

400

Loch na Leitir Beithe

Continued Plodda Falls 2

to Glen Doe (eventually!)

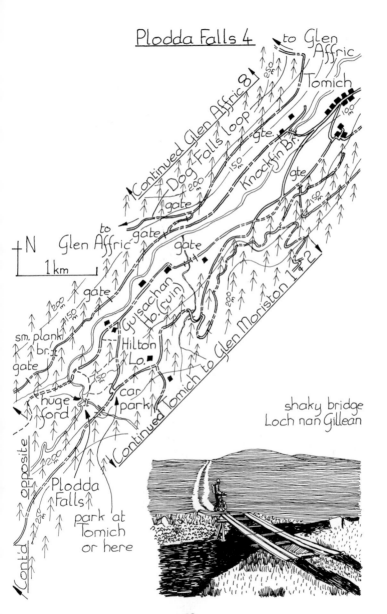

Plodda Falls 4

to Glen Affric

Tomich

Continued Glen Affric 8

Dog Falls loop

Knockfin Br.

gte.

gte

N

1 km

to Glen Affric

gate

gate

gate

gate

Guisachan Ho. (ruin)

sm. plank br.

gate

Hilton Lo.

car park

huge ford

Continued Tomich to Glen Moriston 1 & 2

shaky bridge
Loch nan Gillean

Cont'd opposite

Plodda Falls

park at Tomich or here

33

Glen Affric 1

Glen Affric is the best! The scenery is stunning, the mountainbiking is of the highest order, and the walking suits all standards from pottering-around-the-forest to mountaineering for several successive days – and all based on one glen! Lochs, rivers, waterfalls, and natural pine and birchwoods complete a perfect scene. The glen is popular, and therefore populated, on sunny summer weekends; a forest of signposts entices the non-adventurous away from the car. However, this somewhat spoon-fed scenery is soon left behind in the wilds of the upper glen which boast a youth hostel and a bothy. Connections exist to the west coast via Glen Lichd and to Glen Shiel and Glen Moriston via An Caorann Mor to Cluanie Inn (touching on some exciting routes detailed in Book 8). Lower down the glen is the easy Dog Falls

loop, with its connections to the tracks around Tomich and Plodda Falls; a ride around Loch Beinn a Mheadhoin; and a walker's loop into Gleann nam Fiadh. Shelter is as shown on the page maps, and distances in km (and miles) shown on the page layout set out above.

34

This map is not Glen Affric at all, but its connection to Glen Shiel and Glen Moriston via the Cluanie Inn.

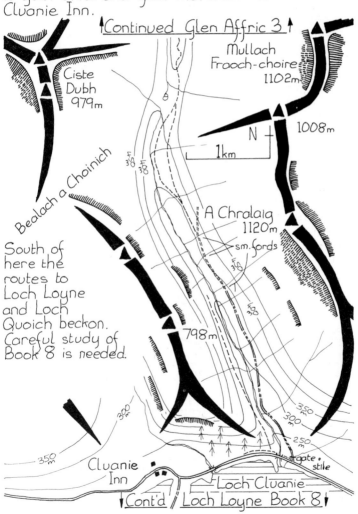

↑ Continued Glen Affric 3 ↑

Mullach Fraoch-choire 1102m

Ciste Dubh 979m

1008m

N

1km

Bealach a Choinich

A Chralaig 1120m

sm. fords

South of here the routes to Loch Loyne and Loch Quoich beckon. Careful study of Book 8 is needed.

798m

Cluanie Inn

gate • stile

Loch Cluanie

↓ Cont'd // Loch Loyne Book 8 ↓

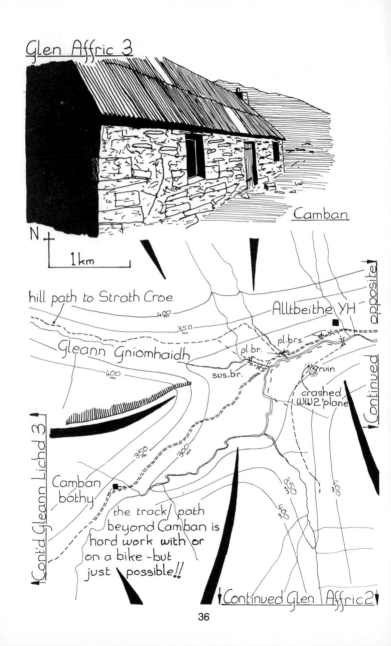

Glen Affric 3

Camban

N
1km

hill path to Strath Croe

Alltbeithe YH

Gleann Gniomhaidh

pl.br.   pl.brs

sus.br.

ruin

crashed
WW2 'plane

Camban
bothy

the track/ path
beyond Camban is
hard work with or
on a bike - but
just possible!!

Cont'd Gleann Lichd 3

Continued opposite

Continued Glen Affric 2

36

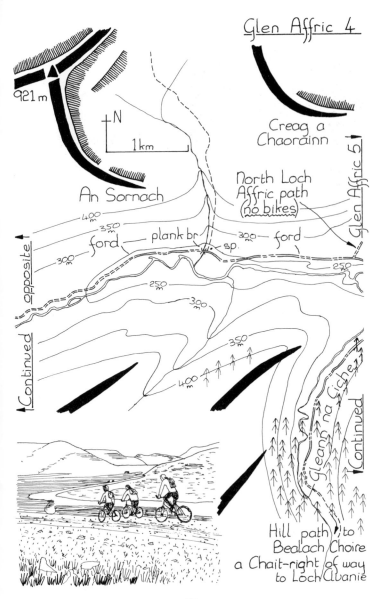

921 m

N

1 km

An Sornach

Creag a Chaorainn

North Loch Affric path (no bikes)

Glen Affric 5

400 m

350 m

ford — plank br

300 m — ford

sp.

300 m

250 m

250 m

opposite ↑

Continued ↑

300 m

350 m

400 m

Gleann na Ciche

Continued

Hill path to Bealach Choire a Chait–right of way to Loch Cluanie

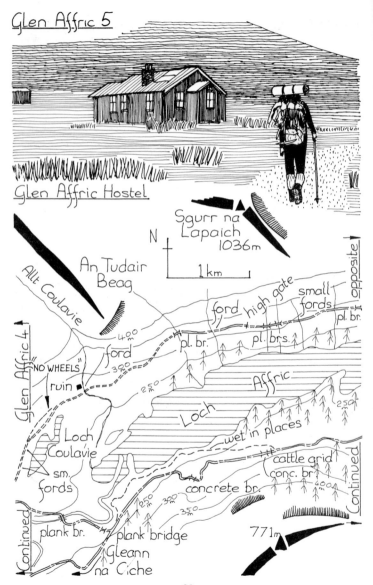

Glen Affric Hostel

Sgurr na Lapaich 1036m

N

1 km

An Tudair Beag

Allt Coulavie

Glen Affric 4

"NO WHEELS"

ruin

ford

400m

300m

250m

ford

pl. br.

ford high gate small fords

pl. br.

pl. brs.

pl. br.

opposite

Affric

250m

Loch

wet in places

Loch Coulavie

sm. fords

250m 300m

350m

concrete br.

cattle grid
conc. br.

400m

Continued

Continued

plank br.

plank bridge
Gleann na Ciche

771m

Continued

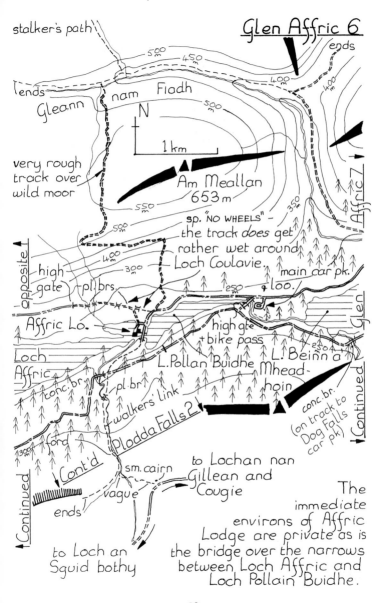

stalker's path

ends

500 m

450 m

400 m

400 m

ends

Gleann   nam   Fiadh

N

500 m

1 km

very rough track over wild moor

Affric 7

550 m

350 m

500 m

Am Meallan 653 m

sp. "NO WHEELS" –
the track *does* get
rather wet around
Loch Coulavie.

400 m

300 m

250 m

main car pk.

opposite ↑

high gate

pl. brs.

loo.

Affric Lo.

high gte
+ bike pass

Glen

Loch Affric

conc. br.

L. Pollan Buidhe

walkers' link

pl. br.

L. Beinn a Mhead- hoin

200 m

Continued →

300 m ford

Plodda Falls 2

conc. br.
(on track to
Dog Falls
car pk)

← Continued

Cont'd

ends

sm. cairn

vague

to Lochan nan Gillean and Cougie

← Continued

to Loch an Squid bothy

The immediate environs of Affric Lodge are private as is the bridge over the narrows between Loch Affric and Loch Pollain Buidhe.

39

Glen Affric 7

This map depicts the link track between the Dog Falls loop and the upper Glen Affric tracks. Cyclists may of course use the quiet(ish) road from the head of the glen as a quicker return to Dog Falls car park – but who is in a hurry to leave Affric? The Dog Falls loop, opposite, provides a link to the extensive tracks around Plodda Falls, which in turn has off-road links much further afield. The area maps on Plodda Falls 2, page 31, and Glen Affric 1, page 34, give an insight into the many possibilities. Several days are needed for thorough exploration.

car park

opposite

Beinn a Mheadhoin 610 m

road

Mheadhoin

Glen Affric 6

Continued

Public

Beinn a

Loch

N

1 km

250 m

Cont'd

Loch a Chlaidheimh

Loch an Eang

Cont'd Plodda Falls 3

350 m
300 m
250 m
350 m
300 m

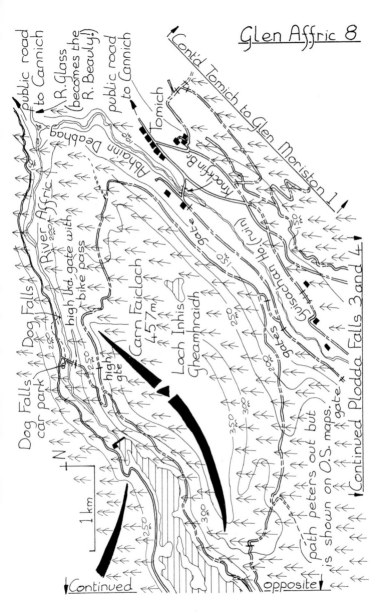

public road to Cannich

R. Glass (becomes the R. Beauly!)

public road to Cannich

Cont'd Tomich to Glen Moriston 1

Tomich

Knockfin Br.

Abhainn Deabhag

Dog Falls

River Affric

Dog Falls

Dog Falls car park

high lkd. gate with bike pass

high gte

Carn Faiclach 457m

Loch Inhis Gheamhraidh

Guisachan Ho! (ruin)

N

1 km

350
300
300
250
250
250
250
200
200
200
150
150
100
50
50

gates

path peters out but is shown on O.S. maps.

gate

Continued Plodda Falls 3 and 4

Continued

opposite

41

Easter Ross

Easter Ross

Access:- This area lies west and north of the towns and villages around the Beauly and Cromarty Firths. Access from the south is via the A9 which now uses the Black Isle as a stepping stone north of the Kessock Bridge, all routes dividing at Tore. However stretches of the old A9 via Beauly, and north of Alness, provide a more interesting drive north.

Accommodation:- In plenty around the Firths; there is a new SYHA hostel in Inverness, another at Strathpeffer, and Carbisdale Castle south of Lairg. Several campsites exist to the east of the region. Further north and west accommodation is limited to B.B's and the occasional isolated hotel.

Geographical Features:- An area of forest, wild moors and long glens with low watersheds enabling many of the tracks to interconnect giving a unique network of off-road routes unequalled anywhere in Scotland.

Mountains:- Ben Wyvis, at 1046m is flanked by the off-road tracks of Torrachilty Forest and Glen Glass, the latter providing access for hillwalkers. Further north and west Gleann Beag penetrates the "Deargs", a range of hills centred around the 1084m Beinn Dearg. Again the tracks in these remote glens give hillwalkers access to the quieter approaches to these hills.

Rivers:- The region is drained by - south to north- the rivers Farrar, Orrin, Conon, Glass, Averon, Carron and Oykel. The crossing of the main tributaries of these rivers can pose problems in the wilder regions; careful study of the detailed maps and local prevailing river

conditions is needed before contemplating long
routes. The Abhainn Poiblidh between Glen
Acholl and Duag Bridge is of particular note.
Forests:- The main forests are Torrachilty
and Morangie; both provide excellent off-
road cycling. Other, quite extensive areas
of forest flank the eastern routes in the
glens though only the above provide usable
networks of tracks.
Lochs:- Lochs Fannich, Glascarnoch and
Vaich have all been raised by hydro dams.
Other significant lochs are Loch Glass, Loch
Garve and Loch Moire.
Emergency:- The long through routes
require a degree of fitness and experience,
and either wild camping or the use of bothies
for full exploration of the region. This is, of
course, the attraction. Less experienced
cyclists are advised to opt for out-and-back
routes (distance to choice) of the easier,
forested regions.

Glen Strathfarrar

- a special note

Possibly conspicuous by its absence from this
guide Glen Strathfarrar is unique. This
27km or 17mile metalled road is controlled by
a manned gate limiting the number of cars
and times of access. A small gate is however
always open for cyclists who may enjoy an
almost traffic free ride to the head of the
glen and back. As the road is metalled a
detailed guide is hardly necessary; suffice
to say that its omission is no excuse for the
the intrepid cyclist to leave Strathfarrar
out of his or her itinerary.

Glen Orrin

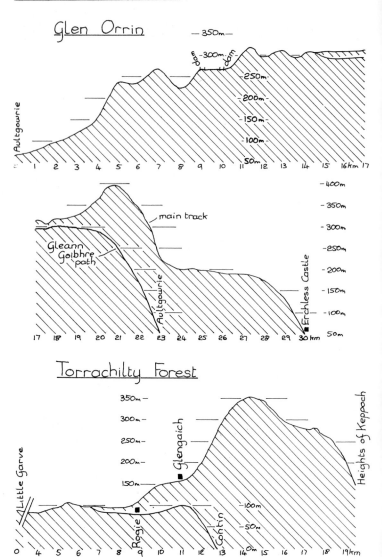

Torrachilty Forest

Strath Vaich/Strath Rannoch

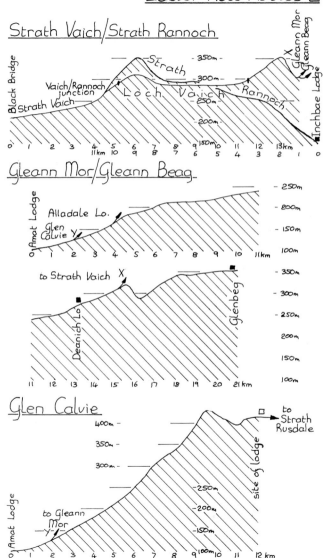

Gleann Mor/Gleann Beag

Glen Calvie

Easter Ross Routes 3

Strath Rusdale

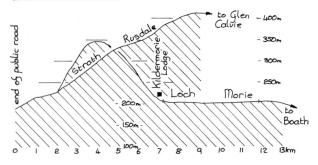

Glen Glass

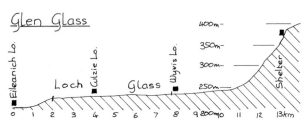

Strath Cuileannach

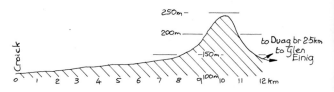

Glen Einig/Strath Mulzie

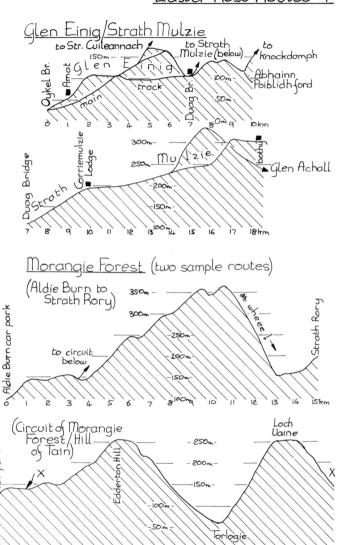

Morangie Forest (two sample routes)

(Aldie Burn to Strath Rory)

(Circuit of Morangie Forest/Hill of Tain)

49

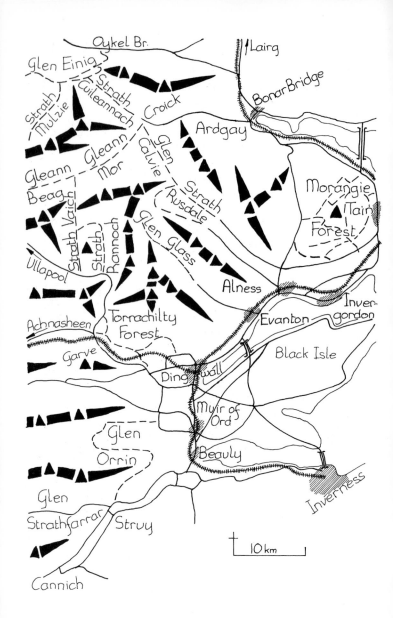

Oykel Br.
Lairg
Glen Einig
Strath Cuileannach
Strath Mulzie
Croick
Bonar Bridge
Ardgay
Glen Calvie
Gleann Mor
Gleann Beag
Strath Rusdale
Morangie Tain Forest
Glen Glass
Strath Vaich
Strath Rannoch
Ullapool
Alness
Inver-gordon
Achnasheen
Torrachilty Forest
Evanton
Black Isle
Garve
Dingwall
Muir of Ord
Glen Orrin
Beauly
Inverness
Glen Strathfarrar
Struy
Cannich

10 km

Glen Orrin 1

The Orrin circuit is best started from Aultgowrie, on the 'back road' between Muir of Ord and Mary-bank. The climb to the dam is metalled, giving a superb long off-road high level traverse and descent - to Erchless. A network of old paths around Gleann Goibhre links ruined farms. There is (rough) shelter as shown on the maps. One way Aultgowrie to Erchless is 29km (18m) and the complete circuit, via Beauly, is 54km (34m). A very satisfying route that "goes somewhere" rather than returning by the same glen. Great!!

Strath Conon

Moy Br.

Marybank

beware! - high locked gate - kissing gate too small for bikes - and a cattle grid!!

50m

100m

Fairburn House

River Orrin

N

150m

1 km

Continued Glen Orrin 3

150m

preferred approach (avoids the environs of Fairburn Ho)

Falls of Orrin gate

100m

Aultgowrie

150m

start

200m

Gleann Goibhre (path)

Allt Goibhre

Muir of Ord
5km/3m

Glen Orrin 2

Since the building of the Orrin dams and the flooding of the lodge (near the head of the reservoir), the head of Glen Orrin has become a very remote place indeed. Access to these upper reaches is via Strath Conon; the reservoir shores are extremely rough going.

444 m

350 m

300 m

empty house
(leaky shelter!) *

Orrin
Reservoir

conc. br.

concrete dam

250

200

collapsed boathouse

earth dam (no shelter)

pole gate

300

300

340 m

N

1 km

opposite

300

Gleann Goibhre

300

hut (shelter)

Allt Goibhre

Continued

animal
shelter

300

350 m

493 m

* I "speak" from
bitter experience!

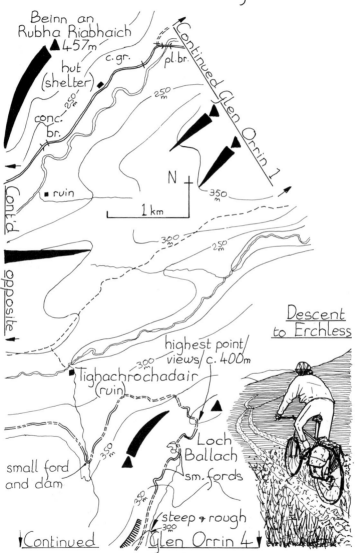

Beinn an
Rubha Riabhaich ▲ 457m

hut (shelter)

c. gr.

pl. br.

Continued Glen Orrin 1

conc. br.

250m

250m

350m

Cont'd opposite

■ ruin

N

1 km

300m

250m

highest point/ views/ c. 400m

300m

Tighachrochadair (ruin)

small ford and dam

350m

Loch Ballach

sm. fords

350m

steep & rough

300m

↓Continued

Glen Orrin 4 ↓

Descent to Erchless

Glen Orrin 4

N
1 km

↑ Continued Glen Orrin 3 ↑

350 m

ford
ford

Beinn a
Chlaonaidh 425m

300

250

ford

200 m

250

sm. ford

Lochan
Fada

A feature of this route is the once-farmed land (and abandoned buildings). An insight into a hard life in times past.

high
gate
stile

high gate

Erchless
Castle

350

250

Bad a
Chlamhain
306m

Erchless
Forest

high gate

high gate

200

150 m

100 m

to
Cannich

A831   to
Beauly →

54

Centred around the forest car park just north of Contin the Torrachilty Forest tracks extend from Little Garve to the N.W. and to the Heights of Keppoch, above the Dingwall to Strathpeffer road. The Garve to Contin section is designated as a cycle route on O.S. maps and serves as a (rather rough) alternative to the busiest and most tortuous stretch of the A835 (using this road as a return from/to Little Garve is not advisable). The further (Forest Enterprise) cycle route to Heights of Keppoch is best completed west to east due to the amount of climbing otherwise involved. Return through Strathpeffer on the A834 is not usually too busy. Little Garve to Contin is 12km or 8m. Contin to H. of K. is 15km or 10m.

Heights of Keppoch to Contin on the road is 10km or 6 miles. Take account of the climb up the main road thro' Strathpeffer. There is no shelter.

Black Water car park and loo.

picnic & park

A835

Little Garve

Black Wtr.

Black Water

Garve

conc. br.

gte

N

1 km

Loch Garve

iron gate

Contd T. For. 2

Torrachilty Forest 2

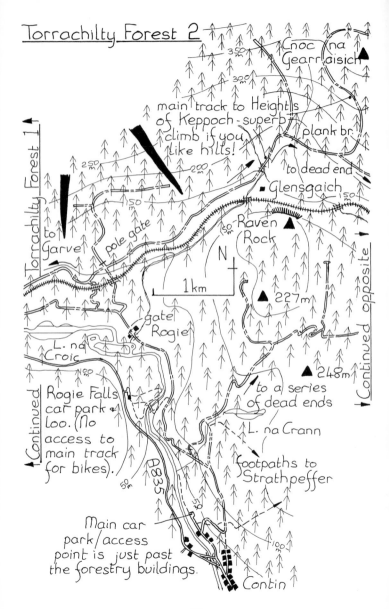

Cnoc na Gearr aisich

350 m

300 m

main track to Heights of Keppoch - superb climb if you like hills!

plank br.

to dead end

250 m

200 m

Glensgaich

150

150 m

Raven Rock

to Garve

pole gate

N

50 m

1 km

227m

gate Rogie

L. na Croic

248m

80 m

to a series of dead ends

Rogie Falls car park & loo. (No access to main track for bikes).

L. na Crann

Footpaths to Strathpeffer

A835

50 m

50

Main car park/access point is just past the forestry buildings.

100 m

Contin

Torrachilty Forest 1

Continued opposite

Continued

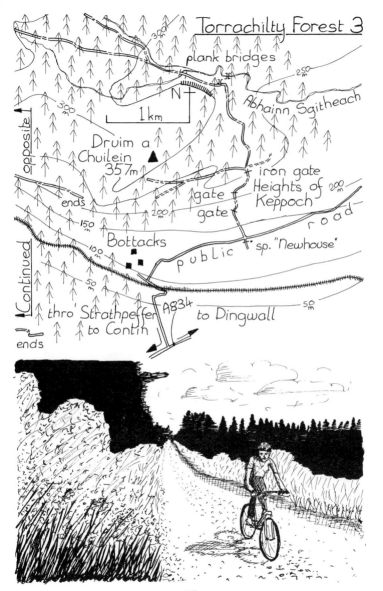

plank bridges

300

250 m

N

1 km

Abhainn Sgitheach

opposite

300

Druim a
Chuilein
357m

iron gate
Heights of
Keppoch

200 m

ends

200

gate

gate

150

road

100

Bottacks

public

sp. "Newhouse"

Continued

50 m

ends

thro' Strathpeffer
to Contin

A834

to Dingwall

50 m

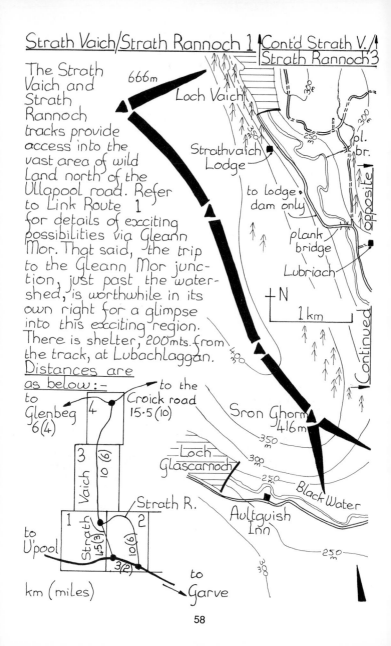

The Strath
Vaich and
Strath
Rannoch
tracks provide
access into the
vast area of wild
land north of the
Ullapool road. Refer
to Link Route 1
for details of exciting
possibilities via Gleann
Mor. That said, the trip
to the Gleann Mor junc-
tion, just past the watershed, is worthwhile in its
own right for a glimpse
into this exciting region.
There is shelter, 200 mts. from
the track, at Lubachlaggan.
<u>Distances are</u>
<u>as below</u>:-

666m

Loch Vaich

Strathvaich
Lodge

to lodge +
dam only

plank
bridge

Lubriach

+N

1 km

to the
Croick road
15.5 (10)

to
Glenbeg
6 (4)

4

3

10 (6)

Vaich

Sron Ghorm
416m

350m

Loch
Glascarnoch

300m

250m

Black Water

Strath R.

1

Strath

4.5 (3)

2

10 (6)

Aultguish
Inn

to
U'pool

3 (2)

to
Garve

250m

30m

km (miles)

Continued

opposite

br.

pl.

300

250m

350m

400

430

ford

397m

350

gate ↑ pr. high gates

↑ stile

Strathrannoch

concrete bridge

Strath

plank bridge

high gate • stile

opposite

350

417m

300

↑N

1 km

Strath

Vaich

Continued

350

300

250

Rannoch

plank bridge

high gate •

kissing gate

sm. plank bridge

300

250

gate • sp.

Druim
Buidhe
c.330m

park

Glascarnoch
River

Black
Bridge

200

high gate

gte.

Inchbae Lodge

If contemplating
the Strath V./Strath R.
circuit it is best to go up the
metalled Strath V. road and
return by the unmade
Strath R. track.

Strath Vaich/Strath Rannoch 3

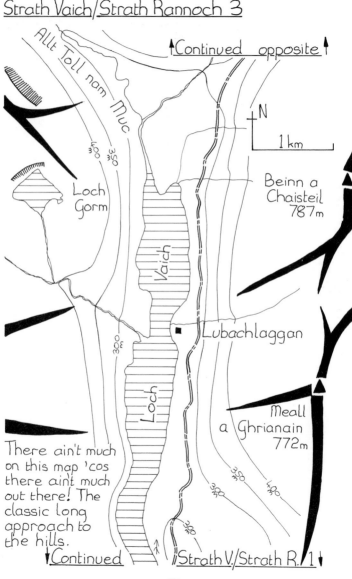

Allt Toll nam Muc

↑ Continued opposite ↑

N

1 km

Loch Gorm

350
350
300

Vaich

300

Beinn a Chaisteil 787m

■ Lubachlaggan

Loch

350
300

Meall a Ghrianain 772m

350
400
300

There ain't much on this map 'cos there ain't much out there! The classic long approach to the hills.

↓ Continued

Strath V./Strath R. 1 ↓

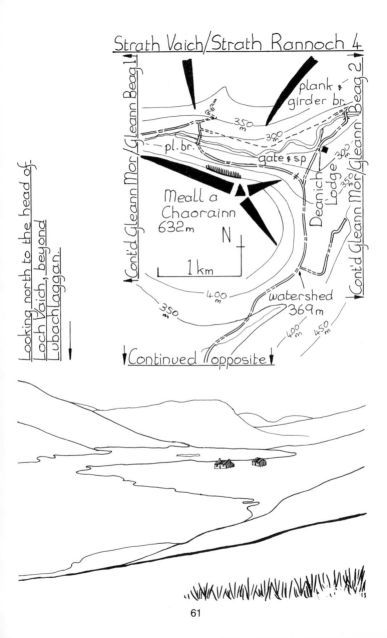

Cont'd Gleann Mór/Gleann Beag 1

Cont'd Gleann Mór/Gleann Beag 2

plank & girder br.

350 m

300

pl. br.

gate & sp

Deanich Lodge

300

350 m

Meall a Chaorainn 632m

N

1 km

Cont'd Gleann Mór/Gleann Beag 2

400 m

watershed 369m

350 m

400 m

450 m

Looking north to the head of Loch Vaich, beyond Lubachlaggan.

↓Continued opposite↓

Gleann Mor/Gleann Beag 1

Gleann Mor and Gleann Beag are accessible
from the minor road to Croick, up Strathcarron
from Ardgay. The start, from Amat Lodge, is
shared with Glen Calvie; thus Gleann Mor not
only links into Strath Vaich, but provides
continuous mountainbiking all the way from
Inchbae Lodge on the Ullapool road to Strath
Rusdale above Alness on the Cromarty Firth.
See Link Route 1 for all the many options.
Amat Lodge to the Strath Vaich junction
is 15·5km (10 miles) and Glenbeg bothy is a
further 6km (4 miles); the last 2km or so is
too rough with (not on!) a bike, believe me -
I've done it!! There is shelter at Glenbeg &
Alladale bothies, however Alladale is a hilly
and rough mile off the main route.
The start is on Gleann Mor/
Gleann Beag 4.

Loch Sruban Mora

735m

opposite

350 m

450 m

400 m

vague but cairned

X

350 m

Continued

vague

Glenbeg bothy

vague

450 m

vague

shallow river crossing

furthest practical point for bikes

N

1 km

X = green post

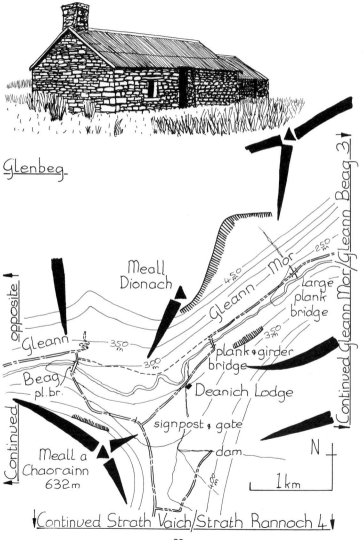

Glenbeg

Continued Gleann Mor/Gleann Beag 3 →

Meall
Dionach

Gleann — Mor

450 m

250 m

large
plank
bridge

Gleann

350 m

300 m

350 m

plank & girder
bridge

← opposite ↑

Beag
pl. br.

Deanich Lodge

signpost & gate

← Continued

Meall a
Chaorainn
632 m

dam

400 m

N

1 km

↓ Continued Strath Vaich/Strath Rannoch 4 ↓

Gleann Mor/Gleann Beag 3

The scene changes completely as the woods
are left behind and the straight, narrow
trench of Gleann Mor is entered. Deanich
Lodge really is in an
isolated location.

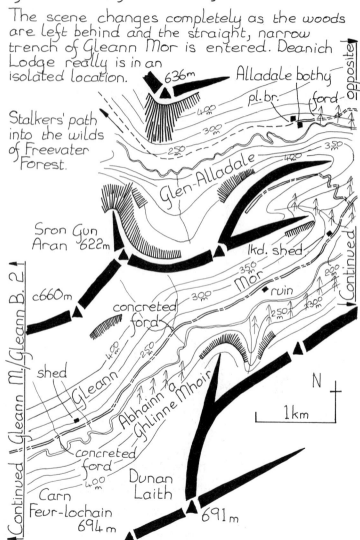

636m

Alladale bothy

pl. br.

ford

Stalkers' path
into the wilds
of Freevater
Forest.

Glen-Alladale

400 m
300 m
250 m
420
350 m

Sron Gun
Aran 622m

lkd. shed

Mor

350 m
300 m

c660m

200

ruin

250 m
300 m

concreted
ford

Gleann

400 m
250 m

shed

Abhainn a
Ghlinne Mhoir

N

1km

concreted
ford

400 m

Carn
Feur-lochain
694m

Dunan
Laith

691m

opposite

Continued

Continued Gleann M./Gleann B. 2

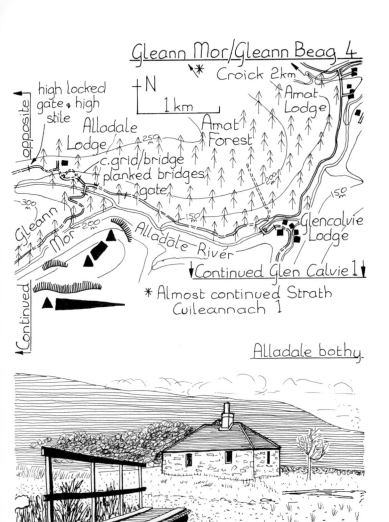

Croick 2km

Amat Lodge

high locked gate · high stile

opposite

Alladale Lodge

Amat Forest

250 m

c.grid/bridge
planked bridges
gate

Glencalvie Lodge

Gleann Mor

300 m

200 m

150 m

Alladale River

150 m

200 m

Continued

Continued Glen Calvie 1

* Almost continued Strath Cuileannach 1

Alladale bothy.

Glen Calvie 1

Glen Calvie links the lower reaches of Gleann Mor with Strath Rusdale. The start, from Amat Lo. on the Croick road, is as for Gleann Mor and Gleann Beag. A left turn is then taken thro' the grounds of Glencalvie Lodge. This part of the route is intrusive, but *is* a right of way. Your author, being old-fashioned considers it a courtesy to dismount and wheel a bike in the close proximity of the lodge and surrounding cottages & outbuildings. This also makes it easier to speak to anyone you may meet..... Tearing along with an "I've a right to cycle anywhere" attitude doesn't help anyone!! - Certainly not the next cyclist! Amat Lodge to Loch a Choirn is 13km (8m), and 22km (14m) thro' to the public road in Strath Rusdale.

Map labels:

Continued Gleann Mor/Gleann Beag 4

pole gte

pr. gts + c.gr.

pl. br.

to Gleann Mor/Beag

Glencalvie Lodge

iron gates

Cnoc na ford Tuppat 438m

c. grid

gte • c.gr.

ft. br.

pl. brs.

pl. brs.

Diebidale

300 m

250 m

300 m

200

300

350 m

400 m

450 m

Glen Diebidale

N

1 km

Continued opposite

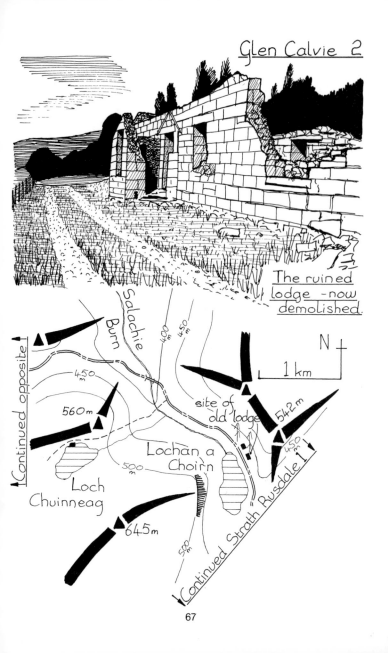

Glen Calvie 2

The ruined
lodge - now
demolished.

Salachie Burn

Continued opposite ↑

400 m
450 m

450 m

N ✛

1 km

site of
old lodge

542 m

450 m

560 m

Lochàn a
Choirn

500 m

Loch
Chuinneag

645 m

500 m

Continued Strath Rusdale ↓

Strath Rusdale 1

A minor road above the Cromarty Firth town of Alness ends in Strath Rusdale at a car park. From the road end a track continues some 19·5km (12m) to Glencalvie Lodge and a further 2·5km (nearly 2m) to the public road at Amat Lodge, near Croick. An out-and-back ride to Lochan a Choirn (9km/6m each way) or the watershed before Glen Calvie (13km/8·5m each way) is feasible. A further alternative return (to Alness) involving some road cycling is via Loch Moire, details of which are on Strath Rusdale 3. Link Route 1 on page 138 illustrates how Strath Rusdale fits into this northern network of connecting glens.

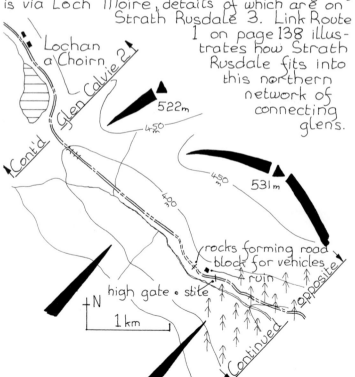

Lochan a Choirn

Glen Calvie 2

Cont'd

522m

450 m

450 m

531m

400 m

rocks forming road block for vehicles

ruin

opposite

high gate • stile

Continued

+N

1 km

Strath Rusdale 2

There is no shelter
in Strath Rusdale
or on the loop track
around Kildermorie
Lodge and Loch
Morie.

Continued opposite

Continued Abhainn Glac an t-Seilirh

350 m

350 m

516m

Bad a
Bhathaich

plank bridges
high gate

Continued Strath Rusdale 3

350 m

350 m

N

1 km

concrete
bridge

300 m

pole gate

Loch Bad
a Bhathaich

Strath Rusdale

gate
conc. bridge
park at end
of public
road

Braeantra

Black Water

250 m

to
Alness
14 km/9m

Strath Rusdale 3

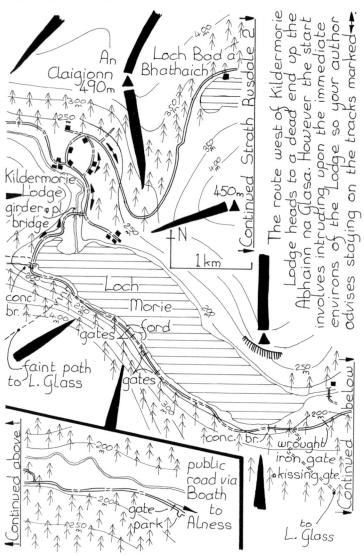

An Claigionn 490m

Loch Bad a Bhathaich

300

250

Continued Strath Rusdale 2

450m

Kildermorie Lodge
girder pl. bridge

N

1 km

Loch Morie ford

concl br.

400

250

gates

faint path to L. Glass

gates

250
300

public road via Boath to Alness

conc. br.

wrought iron gate

kissing gte.

Continued below

to L. Glass

250
300

200

Continued above

200

200

250

gate
park

The route west of Kildermorie Lodge heads to a dead end up the Abhainn na Glasa. However the start involves intruding upon the immediate environs of the Lodge so your author advises staying on the tracks marked.

70

The start of the Glen Glass track (on G.G.3) may seem a little intimidating; imposing lodge gates, barking dogs (big ones!), and the estate office . However, this is a right of way and the trip up to the shelter - the limit for bikes and some 13km or 8miles from the lodge - makes for a superb day out, almost in the shadow of the Ben Wyvis group of mountains. The shelter and the nearby waterfall is an ideal spot for lunch. Walkers' routes exist to Inchbae Lodge hotel on the Ullapool road, some 19km or 12miles from the start;
and also from Wyvis Lodge over to Loch Morie.

Beinn nan Eun
742 m

N

1 km

path peters out in the middle of nowhere!

ford

waterfall

400

the shelter

636 m

300 m

fords

fords

250 m

shaky footbr. 20m up-stream

Loch Bealach Culaidh

350 m

400 m

Glen Glass 2

Continued →

walkers' path peters out, but heads for a clearing thro' the forest above Inchbae Lodge Hotel.

Queen's Cairn
645 m

Glen Glass 2

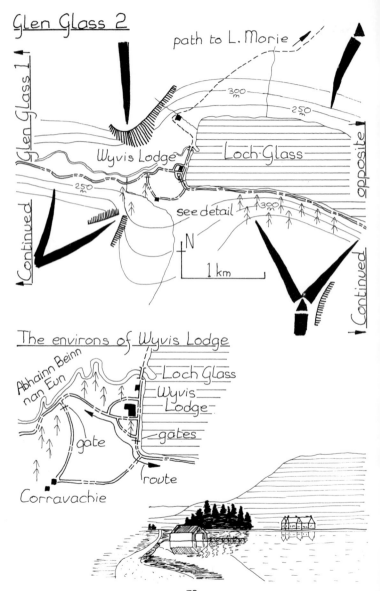

path to L. Morie

Glen Glass 1

300 m

250 m

Wyvis Lodge

Loch-Glass

Continued

opposite

250 m

see detail

300 m

N

1 km

Continued

Continued

The environs of Wyvis Lodge

Abhainn Beinn nan Eun

Loch Glass

Wyvis Lodge

gates

gate

route

Corravachie

72

Glen Glass 3

Meall Mor
738m

Meall Beag
648m

opposite↑

very rough
track to
Loch Morie

Loch

Glass

300

250

300

Continued

Culzie
Lodge

300

250

300

N

1 km

300

Meall na
Drochaide
704 m

300

park/
turn

end of public road
and start at
Eileanach Lodge.
(turn R. after Lo.)

gte.

Strath Cuileannach 1

Strath Cuileannach
is an unremarkable glen
of significant strategic importance
when seen in the context of its many
connections. Running north west from Croick,
and therefore connecting with Glen Calvie,
Gleann Mor/Gleann Beag and on into Strath
Vaich and Strath Rannoch, its north western
end runs into Glen Einig/Strath Mulzie which
in turn lead on to Glen Achall and Ullapool.
Link Route 1 on page 138 explains. Croick
to Duag Bridge is some 15km or 9·5 miles,
and Croick to Oykel Bridge is 17km or 10·5
miles. The climb over to Glen Einig is
rough going but only for about 500 metres.
There is shelter, some distance off the track,
above, plus a motley collection of tin sheds
along the route as indicated may provide
temporary respite from the elements.

Strath Cuileannach 2

Croick church

484 m

481 m

opposite ↑

Continued ↑

gate
concrete br.
tin shed
old fm. bldgs.
gate

gate
tin shed
concrete br.
gate
shed

gate

c. grid ⚬ gate

Strath Cuileannach

250 m
150 m
200 m
150 m
200 m

↑N

1 km

200 m

250 m
300 m

557 m

Abhainn an t-Strath
Chuileannaich

tin sheds

high
gate

park

Croick

Croick Church

75

Glen Einig/Strath Mulzie 1

Glen Einig and Strath Mulzie combine to provide one of the most exciting routes in the area. Glen Einig ties together Oykel Bridge - at its start, on Glen E./Strath M. 4 - Strath Cuileannach; and has important connections with Glen Achall - the thro' route to Ullapool on the

Mullach a Bhrian Leitir

400

350

300

Continued Glen Achall 4.

Glen Duchray

Lochan Badan Glaslaith

↑ N

1 km

400

450m

350m

Continued opposite

ends

Meall nam Bradham 677m

west coast. Link Route 1 refers. The afforestation at the start gives way to a wild glen under the northern crags of one of the remotest mountains in Scotland - Seana Bhraigh. Coiremor, a small bothy, nestles at its foot. Several small fords, one large ford (avoidable by a bridge), and one seriously large ford have to be negotiated in order to reach the bothy. A suspension bridge (if you call two strands of wire a bridge!) avoids the largest fords. Your author prefers to paddle. Oykel Bridge to Duag Bridge is 7km or 4.5 miles. Duag Bridge to the bothy is a further 11km or 7 miles. There is shelter at Duag Br. and the bothy, Coiremor. Take care at those fords. This route is one of the best!!

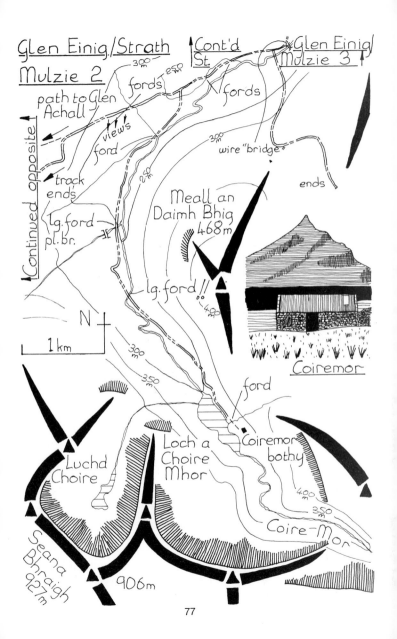

300 m

250 m

fords

fords

path to Glen Achall

views

ford

300 m

wire "bridge"

ends

Continued opposite

track ends'

250 m

lg. ford pl. br.

Meall an Daimh Bhig 468m

N

1 km

lg. ford!!

400 m

Coiremor

300 m

350 m

ford

Luchd Choire

Loch a Choire Mhor

Coiremor bothy

Coire-Mor

400 m

350 m

Seana Bhraigh 927m

906m

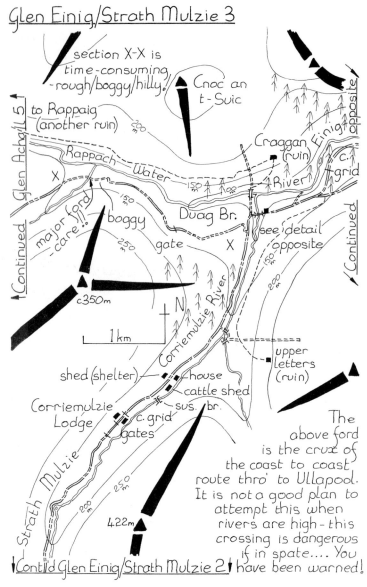

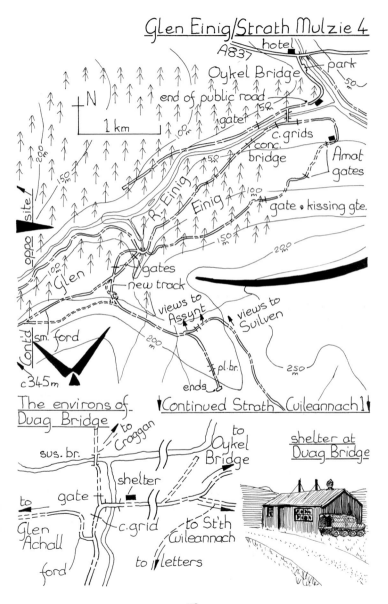

Glen Einig/Strath Mulzie 4

A837   hotel

Oykel Bridge   park   50

end of public road

gate   150 m

c. grids

conc. bridge

Amat gates

N

1 km

200 m

150 m

100 m

site

oppo site

R. Einig   Einig   100

gate • kissing gte.

150

Glen   100   200

gates

new track

views to Assynt   views to Suilven

Contd   sm. ford   200   250 m

c 345 m

pl. br.

ends

Continued Strath Cuileannach 1

The environs of Duag Bridge

to Croggan

sus. br.

to Oykel Bridge

shelter

to Glen Achall

gate

c. grid

to St'th Cuileannach

ford

to letters

shelter at Duag Bridge

Morangie Forest 1

Morangie Forest offers a huge variety, and several days out for the mountain biker. There are new forest tracks, older forest tracks, bits of old "roads" and several connecting stretches of minor road joining the various "entry points" to the forest. The tracks range in height from virtually sea level to over 1000'. Try to avoid cycling on the busy A9, though the A836 is not too unpleasant if used to connect the forest tracks. Distances are obviously to choice and a simplified(!) page plan/distance chart is set out below; distances are given in km only. The main car park is at Aldie Burn. The only shelter is at Coag.

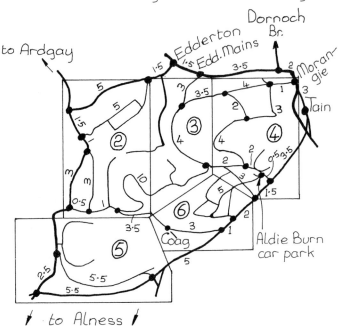

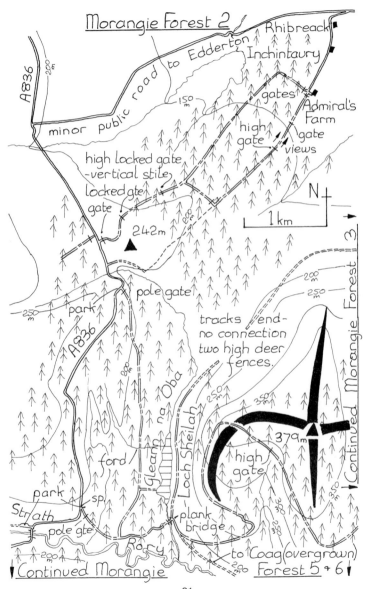

Morangie Forest 2

A836

200 m

minor public road to Edderton

Rhibreack

Inchintaury

150 m

gates

high gate

Admiral's Farm

gate

views

high locked gate
-vertical stile

locked gate

gate

242m ▲

N+

1 km

pole gate

park

A836

tracks end-
no connection
two high deer
fences.

200 m

250 m

Continued Morangie Forest 3

Gleann na Oba

Loch Sheilah

250 m

250 m

350 m

379m ▲

high gate

350 m

ford

park

sp

Strath

pole gte

Rory

plank
bridge

to Coag (overgrown)

350 m

200 m

200 m

Continued Morangie

Forest 5 & 6

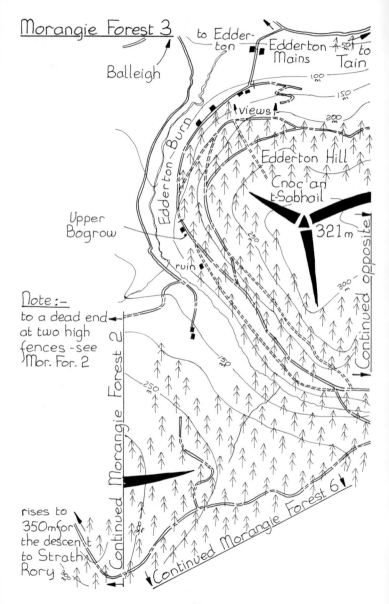

Morangie Forest 3

to Edder-
ton

Edderton
Mains

to
Tain

Balleigh

views

Edderton Hill

Cnoc an
t-Sabhail

321m

Upper
Bogrow

ruin

Edderton Burn

Continued opposite

Note :-
to a dead end
at two high
fences - see
Mor. For. 2

Continued Morangie Forest 2

Continued Morangie Forest 6

rises to
350m for
the descent
to Strath
Rory

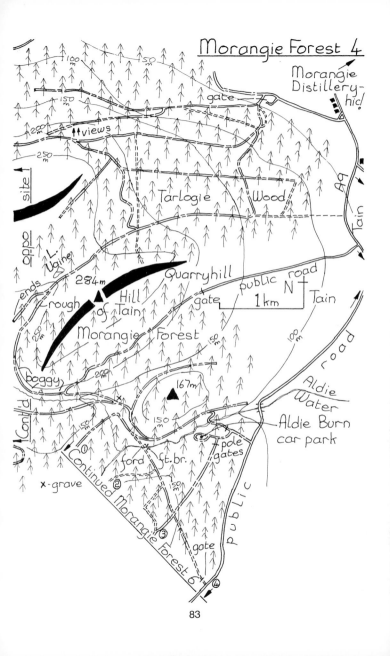

Morangie
Distillery-
hic!

gate

views

Tarlogie   Wood

site

oppo

L.
Ugine

ends

284m

rough

Hill
of Tain

Quarryhill

public road   N

1 km   Tain

Morangie Forest

boggy

167m

(Cont'd)

Aldie
Water

Aldie Burn
car park

x ×

ford f.br.

pole
gates

①

x-grave   ②

Continued Morangie Forest 6

③

gate

④

public

road

A9

Tain

100m
150m
200m
250m
200m
200m
50m
100m
150m
150m

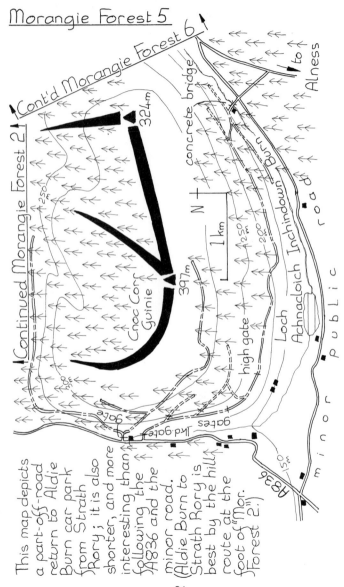

Cont'd Morangie Forest 6

Continued Morangie Forest 2

324 m

Cnoc Corr Guinie

397 m

N

1 km

concrete bridge

high gate

gates

L'kd gates

gate

Loch Achnacloich

Inchindown Burn

minor Public road

to Alness

A836

150 m

This map depicts a part-off-road return to Aldie Burn car park from Strath Rory; it is also shorter, and more interesting than following the A836 and the minor road. (Aldie Burn to Strath Rory is best by the hill route at the foot of "Mor. Forest 2".)

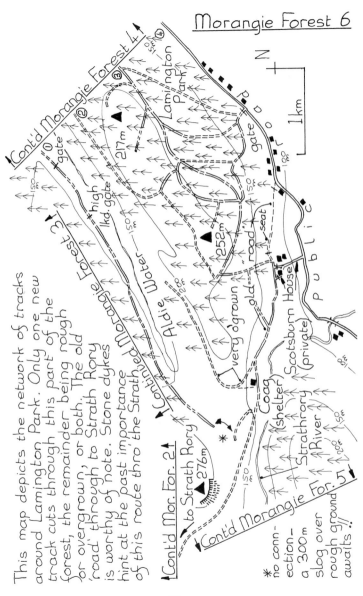

This map depicts the network of tracks around Lamington Park. Only one new track cuts through this part of the forest, the remainder being rough for overgrown, or both. The old 'road' through to Strath Rory is worthy of note. Stone dykes hint at the past importance of this route thro' the Strath.

N

1km

Cont'd Morangie Forest 4

Cont'd Morangie Forest 3

Cont'd Moor. For. 2

Cont'd Mor. For. 2

Cont'd Morangie For. 5

Lamington Park

② ③ ④

① gate

gate

217m

high lkd. gate

Aldie Water

252m

seat

very'dgrown

"old" "road"

Scotsburn House (private)

Coag (shelter)

Strathrory River

to Strath Rory 276m

Public

* no connection— a 300m slog over rough ground awaits∴

Wester Ross

Wester Ross

Access:- This large and complex area lies north of Glen Shiel and south of Ledmore junction and Glen Oykel. It encompasses the western half of a huge tract of wild land crossed only by the Garve-Achnasheen and Garve to Braemore junction roads. Access is therefore a slow and tortuous affair; from Inverness via Garve and either the A832 or A835, or from the south via Shiel Bridge. The rewards are, however, proportional to the effort required to explore this exciting region.

Accommodation:- The most useful hostels are Ullapool, Torridon and Ratagan. A fairly even sprinkling of private hostels, bunkhouses, campsites, B&B's and hotels pepper the west coast, but inland even the main roads cross large remote areas with only the odd isolated B&B or hotel. There are many self-catering cottages on the coast.

Geographical Features:- A wild, indented, fjord-like coastline gives way to deep glens and high mountains. The watershed is well to the west so despite the location of the region much of the water drains to the east. There is little flat ground for cultivation.

Mountains:- Torridon, An Teallach, Slioch, Beinn Dearg, Sgurr Mor, The Five Sisters, Carn Eige.... far too many to single out the "best".... oh yes : The Fisherfield Forest..... I could go on (and on!), but (no doubt to your relief!) I won't. Suffice to say if you like mountains and wild country this region is a dream, if you don't you shouldn't be here... and why are you reading this?

Rivers:- Almost a repeat of my notes on

Easter Ross as most are fed by or originate from burns in the west. Flowing west are the Rhidorroch River(in Glen Achall), Gruinard R., River Torridon, River Carron and River Shiel to mention a few of the main, albeit short, Atlantic-bound rivers.

Forests:- Apart from Gleann Udalain with its surprisingly good biking there is little forestry - hence generally fewer good mountain-biking routes given the huge extent of this region.

Lochs:- Here this area really scores! Sea lochs Loch Broom, Little Loch Broom, Loch Ewe, Loch Gairloch, Loch Torridon, Loch Carron, Loch Alsh and Loch Duich reach inland like fjords. Inland Loch Achall, Loch na Sealga and Loch Damh are all pleasant stretches of water whilst Loch Maree (formerly another Loch Ewe) is the finest, with its classic view of Slioch. A path alongside Mullardoch is included but Lochs Monar, Mullardoch and Affric belong with the eastbound rivers. Loch Fannich is a reservoir and forms a part of the Fannich/Glascarnoch/Vaich hydro scheme. Small "fishing" lochs abound - too numerous to mention. Fionn Loch is a wonderful sheet of water but the landowner has yet to be convinced that the word "access" also includes, by definition, cyclists.

Emergency:- Only three locations may give rise to problems for the unwary: The Glen Achall/Glen Einig connection which includes a major ford; the head of Loch Fannich which is very remote; and the Gleann Lichd/Affric connection which is both remote and hard going with a bike. Refer to Link Routes and study the page maps. Care is required!

Wester Ross Routes 1

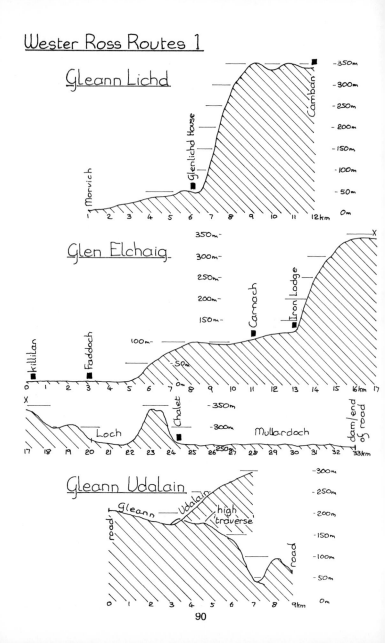

Gleann Lichd

Morvich · Glenlichd House · Camban
(elevation profile, 0–12 km, 0m–350m)

Glen Elchaig

Killilan · Faddoch · Carnach · Iron Lodge · X
(elevation profile, 0–17 km, 0m–350m)

X · Loch · Chalet · Mullardoch · dam/end of road
(elevation profile, 17–33 km, 250m–350m)

Gleann Udalain

road · Gleann · Udalain · high traverse · road
(elevation profile, 0–9 km, 0m–300m)

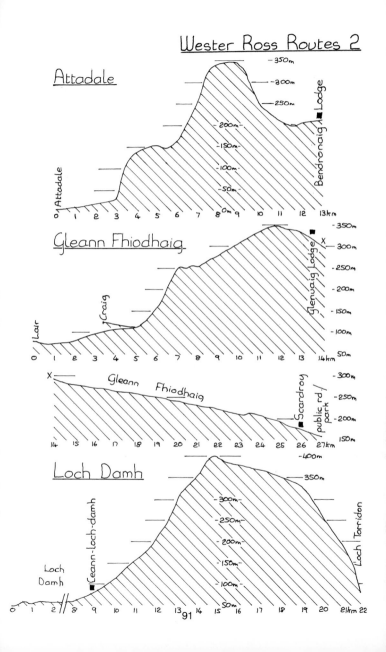

Wester Ross Routes 2

Attadale

Gleann Fhiodhaig

Loch Damh

Wester Ross Routes 3

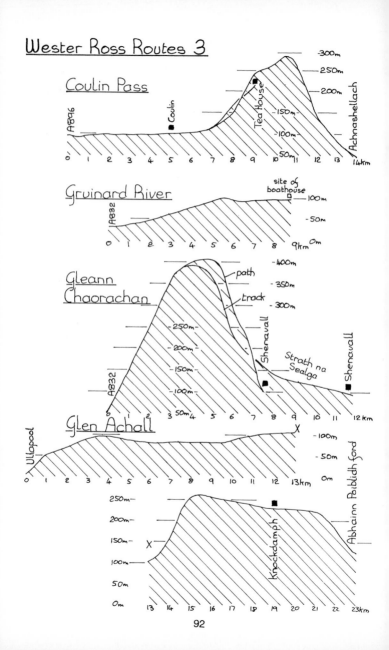

Coulin Pass

300m, 250m, 200m, 150m, 100m, 50m

A896 — Coulin — Tea House — Achnashellach

0 1 2 3 4 5 6 7 8 9 10 11 12 13 14km

Gruinard River

site of boathouse — 100m, 50m, 0m

A832

0 1 2 3 4 5 6 7 8 9km

Gleann Chaorachan

400m, 350m, 300m, path, track, 250m, 200m, 150m, 100m, 50m

A832 — Shenavall — Strath na Sealga — Shenavall

0 1 2 3 4 5 6 7 8 9 10 11 12km

Glen Achall

Ullapool — X — 100m, 50m, 0m — Abhainn Poiblidh ford

0 1 2 3 4 5 6 7 8 9 10 11 12 13km

250m, 200m, 150m, 100m, 50m, 0m

X — Knockdamph

13 14 15 16 17 18 19 20 21 22 23km

92

Loch Fannich

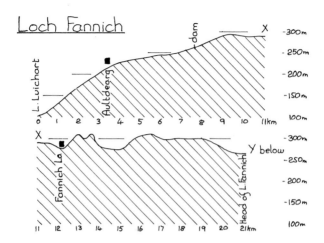

Lochrosque Forest

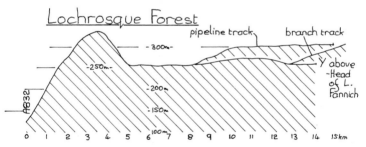

Gleann Lichd 1

Just north of Shiel Bridge Gleann Lichd cuts a deep trough heading in a south easterly direction behind the Five Sisters of Kintail to the bealach. Further north lie Sgurr a Choire Ghairbh, Meall an Fhuarain Mhoir and Ben Attow. Here it is possible to walk or cycle in the company of some imposing mountains. The glen provides a west coast connection into Glen Affric, the head of which is surrounded by even higher summits. The through route is, however, extremely rough to cycle - from Glenlicht House to about a mile west of Camban bothy - a distance of 4·5km or 3 miles -

best done east to west by bike. Glenlicht Ho. is a locked climbing hut with a tiny open bothy at one end. The next shelter is at Camban in Glen Affric. The start to Glenlicht Ho. is only about 6km or 4miles; half a day or an evening is ample time with a bike.

Glenlicht House

95

Gleann Lichd 2

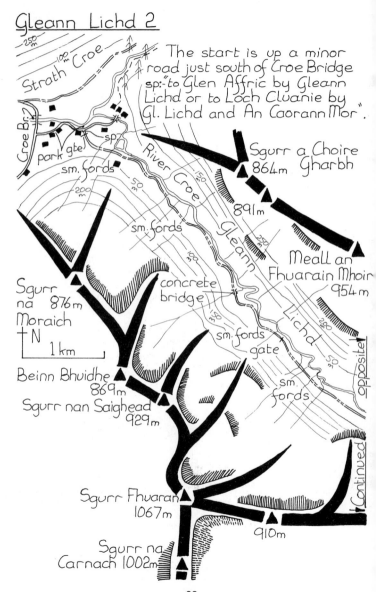

The start is up a minor road just south of Croe Bridge sp: "to Glen Affric by Gleann Lichd or to Loch Cluanie by Gl. Lichd and An Caorann Mor".

250m

100m

Strath Croe

Croe Br.?

park gte

sp

River Croe

50

150

sm. fords

200m

Sgurr a Choire Gharbh 864m

891m

Gleann

250

Meall an Fhuarain Mhoir 954m

sm. fords

100

concrete bridge

Sgurr na 876m Moraich

150

Lichd

280

N

1 km

sm. fords

gate

50

Beinn Bhuidhe 869m

Sgurr nan Saighead 929m

sm. fords

Continued opposite

Sgurr Fhuaran 1067m

910m

Sgurr na Carnach 1002m

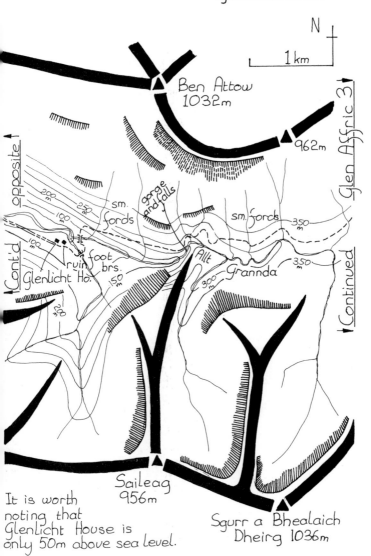

N

1 km

Ben Attow
1032m

962m

Glen Affric 3

opposite ↑

200 m

250 m

sm. fords

gorge and falls

sm. fords

350 m

100 m

100 m

ruin

Glenlicht Ho.

foot brs.

50

200 m

Cont'd ↓

Allt Grannda

300 m

350 m

Continued ↓

Saileag
956m

Sgurr a Bhealaich
Dheirg 1036m

It is worth
noting that
Glenlicht House is
only 50m above sea level.

Glen Elchaig 1

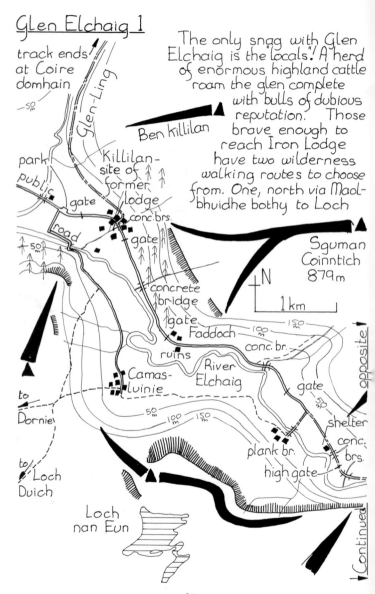

The only snag with Glen Elchaig is the "locals"! A herd of enormous highland cattle roam the glen complete with bulls of dubious reputation. Those brave enough to reach Iron Lodge have two wilderness walking routes to choose from. One, north via Maol-bhuidhe bothy to Loch

track ends at Coire domhain

Glen-Ling

Ben killilan

park

public

road

gate

Killilan-site of former lodge

conc. brs.

gate

concrete bridge

gate

Faddoch

conc. br.

ruins

River Elchaig

Camas-luinie

Sguman Coinntich 879 m

N

1 km

gate

shelter

conc. brs.

to Dornie

to Loch Duich

plank br.

high gate

conc. brs.

Loch nan Eun

opposite

Continued

Monar, the second, due west tracing a vague stalkers' path north of the head of Loch Mullardoch, then by an even rougher path along the north shore to the dam.

Iron Lodge is 13 km (8 m) from Killilan, Mullardoch dam is a further 21 km or 13 miles.

Heavy-duty seat!

opposite ↑

410 m

N

1 km

150 m 200 m

Loch na...

Leitreach

Continued Glen Elchaig

Continued

50 m

150 m 100 m

200 m

730m

Falls of Glomach

<u>Note:-</u>
The path to Strath Croe via the Falls of Glomach.

path to Strath Croe

Glen Elchaig 3

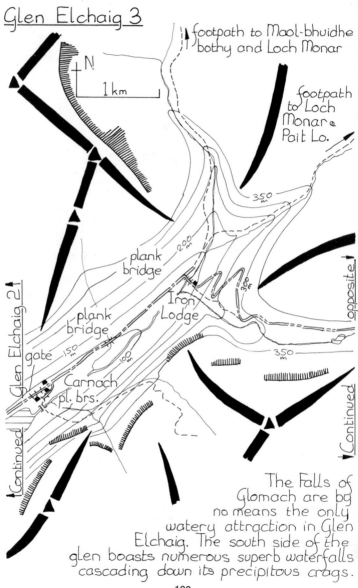

footpath to Maol-bhuidhe bothy and Loch Monar

footpath to Loch Monar & Pait Lo.

N

1 km

350 m

200 m

plank bridge

opposite

Iron Lodge

plank bridge

300 m

Glen Elchaig 2

gate 150 m

100 m

350 m

Continued

Carnach pl. brs.

Continued

The Falls of Glomach are by no means the only watery attraction in Glen Elchaig. The south side of the glen boasts numerous superb waterfalls cascading down its precipitous crags.

100

The track ends in some of the wildest country imaginable. The two glens to the south end at the great north Affric ridge, topped by Sgurr nan Ceathreamhnan - a mountain almost as complex, and grand, as its name.

▲ 678m

← opposite

400 m

350 m

ruin ■ 250

Loch Mullardoch

Glen Elchaig 5 →

← Continued

→ Continued

N

300

350 m

pt.br.

400 m

1km

Gleann Sithidh

Mullach na Dheiragain

▲ 973m

old path to Glen

Gleann a Choilich

Affric

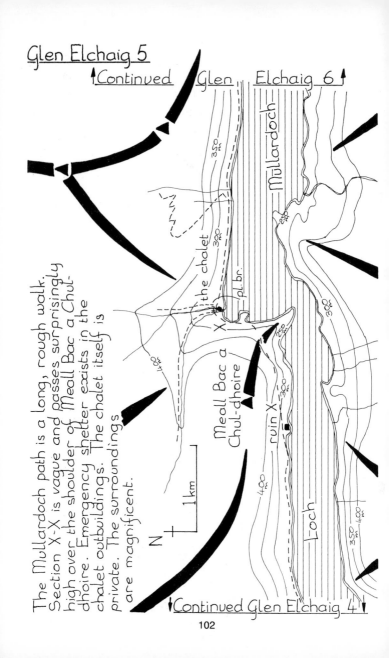

The Mullardoch path is a long, rough walk. Section X-X is vague and passes surprisingly high over the shoulder of Meall Bac a Chul-dhoire. Emergency shelter exists in the chalet outbuildings. The chalet itself is private. The surroundings are magnificent.

N

1 km

the chalet

pl. br.

Meall Bac a Chul-dhoire

ruin X

Mullardoch

Loch

350 m

300 m

400

400

300

350 m

300 m

↓Continued Glen Elchaig 4↓

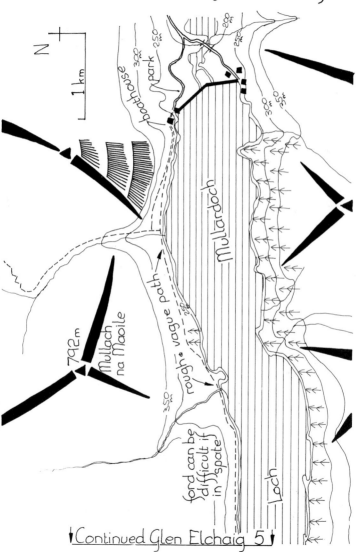

N

1 km

boathouse

x park

250 m

200 m

250 m

300 m

350 m

Mullardoch

792 m
Mullach
na Maoile

rough vague path

350 m

ford can be
difficult if
in spate

Loch

↓ Continued Glen Elchaig 5 ↓

Gleann Udalain 1

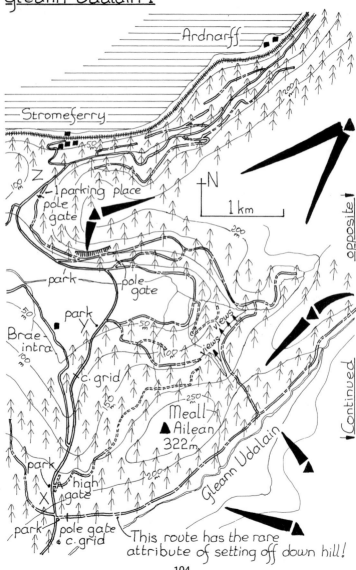

Ardnarff

Stromeferry

N

1 km

opposite

Continued

parking place
pole gate

park
pole gate

park

Brae-intra

park X

c. grid

views

Meall
Ailean
322m

Gleann Udalain

park

high gate
X

park
pole gate
c. grid

This route has the rare
attribute of setting off down hill!

Gleann Udalain 2

The Gleann Udalain tracks provide surprisingly good mountainbiking - much better than a casual glance at the O.S. map would suggest. The best starting point is probably point X on the map opposite. Gleann Udalain may then be explored to its limit, then a partial return brings you to the start of the high level traverse track -mostly downhill- so midge-beating speeds can be maintained throughout! The many dead-ends can be ignored and the track followed north to just above Stromeferry at point Z. The ride back up the road is a bit of a slog but this can be reduced by starting at the huge lay-by at point Y (thus spoiling that downhill start!) The round trip is 14km or 9miles; the trip up to the head of Gleann Udalain adds 8km or 5 miles return. An ideal sortie for half a day or a summer evening. There is no shelter.

387m

300 m

c335m

opposite ↑

ford

250 m

250 m

316m

pathless right-of-way to Glen Ling

N

1 km

↑Continued

Attadale 1

The track to Bendronaig Lodge initially follows the River Attadale (after passing the gardens) and strikes out over moors to descend to the Black Water which is a continuation of Glen Ling. However, the Glen Ling track is not continuous, ending at Coire-domhain. Bendronaig Lodge marks one of those wonderful wilderness "junctions". The pathless Glen Ling right-of-way meets the above track, and paths lead north to Bearneas (and eventually Gleann

Attadale House

cgrs

gate   cattle grid

Strathan   locked gate   girder   plank bridge

concrete bridge

Carn Ruairidh 378m

River Attadale

363m

pl. br.

pl. brs.

335m   1km

N

Loch an Iasaich

better down than up!

Continued opposite !

Fhiodhaig via Bealach Bhearnais), and east via Loch Calavie to Pait Lodge. Attadale to Bendronaig Lodge is 13·5 km or 8·5 miles. There is shelter in the bothy at the lodge.

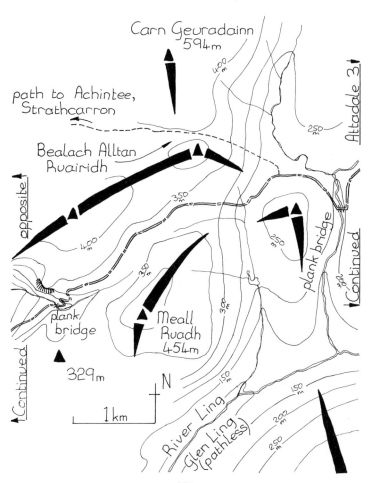

Carn Geuradainn
594m

path to Achintee, Strathcarron

Bealach Alltan Ruairidh

Attadale 3

opposite

plank bridge

Continued

Continued

plank bridge

Meall Ruadh
454m

329m

N

1 km

River Ling

Glen Ling (pathless)

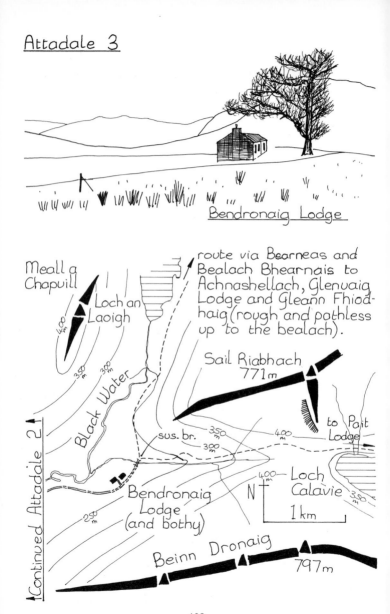

Bendronaig Lodge

Meall a Chapuill

Loch an Laoigh

400
350m 300m

Black Water

route via Bearneas and Bealach Bhearnais to Achnashellach, Glenuaig Lodge and Gleann Fhiodhaig (rough and pathless up to the bealach).

Sail Riabhach 771m

to Pait Lodge

sus. br.

350
300

400

N

Loch Calavie

400m

350

1 km

Bendronaig Lodge (and bothy)

250m

Continued Attadale 2

Beinn Dronaig 797m

Gleann Fhiodhaig 1

This route extends from Achnashellach in the
west to the head of Strathconon. If cycling the
best direction is from west to east as the climbing
is done on good tracks, and the rough section (here
a bike is more of a hindrance than an aid to progress) is covered with a slightly favourable
gradient. Use of a bike east of Glenuaig Lodge
cannot be encouraged in other than dry conditions due to erosion caused by cycle tyres; in
the wet this section should be walked. The
total distance from Achnashellach to Scardroy
at the head of Strathconon is about 27km or
17miles. Starting at Craig saves some 5km
or 3miles. The short route (one way) from
Craig to Glenuaig Lodge is 10km or 6miles.
Achnashellach has a railway station making
a hard day out from here to Muir of Ord
station a possibility - adding some 40km or 25

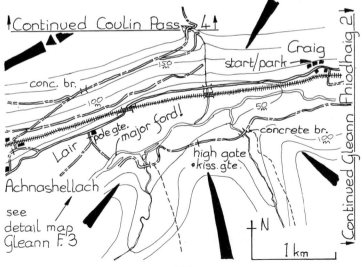

↑Continued Coulin Pass 4↑

conc. br.

150m

100m

Lair

pole gte.   major ford!

Craig
start/park

50m

concrete br.

100m

high gate
• kiss. gte.

Achnashellach

see
detail map
Gleann F. 3

↑N

1 km

→Continued Gleann Fhiodhaig 2
←Continued Gleann Fhiodhaig

Gleann Fhiodhaig 2

Fhiodhaig 1

(Cont'd Glean)

150m
100m
200m
250m
300m

high gate
concrete brs.

conc. br.

200m

250m
m

Meall an Fhliuchaird 405m

300m

high gate, kissing gate & s.p.

sus. br.

450m
350m
300m
350m

450m
350m
m

opposite

Continued

miles of road cycling to an already arduous day. The wide but usually shallow ford at Lair saves the road walk/cycle to Craig from Achnashellach station. The only shelter is an outbuilding at Glenuaig Lo. This route is best kept for a fine day!

single wire!

2-wire bridge/ford

350m
m

N+

1 km

862m

Sgurr na Feartaig

Bealach Bhearnais

path ends – views to Skye!

Sgurr Choinnich 978m

pathless rough route to Bearneas

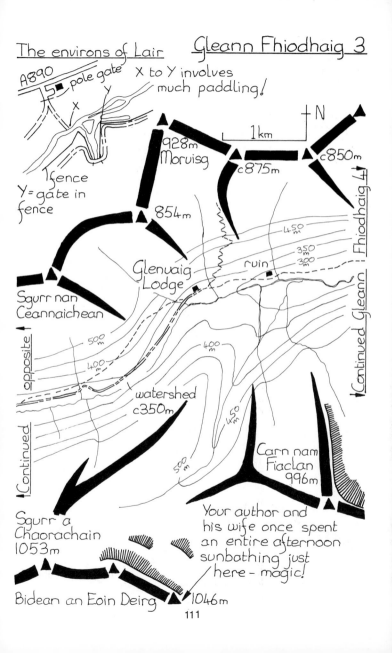

A890

5 pole gate

X to Y involves
much paddling!

X   Y

1km   N

fence

Y = gate in
fence

928m
Moruisg

c875m

c850m

854m

Continued Gleann Fhiodhaig 4

450 m

350 m

300 m

Glenuaig
Lodge

ruin

Sgurr nan
Ceannaichean

opposite

500 m

400 m

400 m

watershed
c350m

450 m

Continued

500 m

Carn nam
Fiaclan
996m

Sgurr a
Chaorachain
1053m

Your author and
his wife once spent
an entire afternoon
sunbathing just
here - magic!

Bidean an Eoin Deirg   1046m

Gleann Fhiodhaig 4

Glenuaig Lodge

867m
Carn Gorm
875m

Meall Doir
a Bhainne 653m

Cont'd G.Fhiodhaig 3

N

1km

Gleann Fhiodhaig

400 m

450 m

350 m

River Meig

250 m

Continued opposite

350 m

400 m

450 m

627m

Creag
Dhubh Mhor 854m

Creag
Dubh Beag

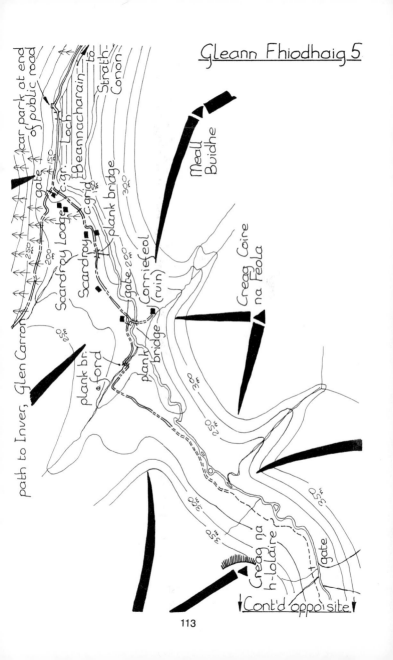

car park at end of public road

gate

to Strath-Conon

Loch Beannacharain

150

200

Meall Buidhe

Scardroy Lodge

Scardroy c.gr.

c.gr.

plank bridge

200

250

300

gate 200

Corriefeol (ruin)

250

Creag Coire na Feola

path to Inver, Glen Carron

200

plank br. & ford

250

Plank bridge

300

250

300

350

Creag na h-Iolaire

gate

↓ Cont'd opposite ↓

Loch Damh 1

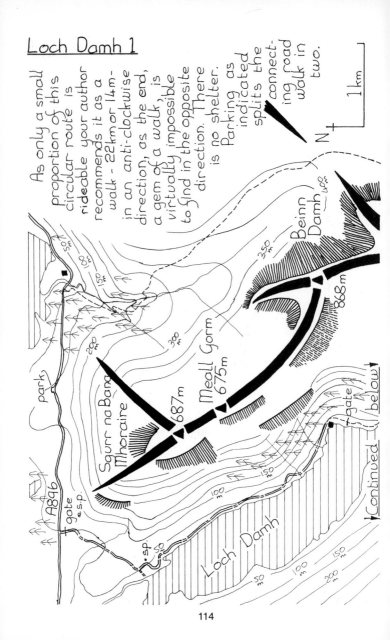

As only a small proportion of this circular route is rideable your author recommends it as a walk – 22km or 14km – in an anti-clockwise direction, as the end, a gem of a walk, is virtually impossible to find in the opposite direction. There is no shelter. Parking as indicated splits the connecting road walk in two.

N↑

1 km

Beinn Damh 400m
868m

Meall Gorm 675m

Sgurr na Bana Mhoraire
687m
300m
250m
200m

park

A896

gate e.s.p.

s.p.

50m 100m 150m 200m

Loch Damh

gate

◄ Continued below ►

114

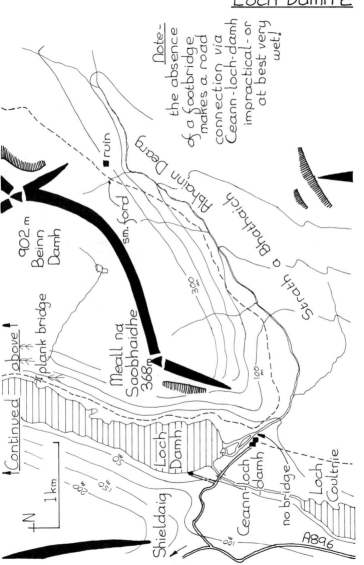

Note -
the absence of a footbridge makes a road connection via Ceann-loch-damh impractical - or at best very wet!

ruin

Abhainn Dearg

sm. ford

902 m
Beinn Damh

Srath a Bhathaich

300

plank bridge

Continued above ↑
above ↑

Meall na Saobhaidhe 368m

100

+N
1 km

Loch Damh

50
150
200

Shieldaig

Ceann-loch-damh

no bridge

Loch Coultrie

A896

100

Coulin Pass 1

The Coulin Pass links Glen Torridon with Glen Carron, running from Loch Clair (with its classic view of Liathach) in the north to Achnashellach Station in the south, a distance of some 14km or 9 miles. The track appears from the O.S. map to be continuous but the route is signposted around the path on the north east shore of Loch Coulin. This is an inconvenience for cyclists who have to wheel their bikes for about half of this mercifully short (about a mile) section. The track rises to its 286m summit just above Glen Carron, the northern half of the route being virtually level. A diversion to the tea-house and its neighbouring waterfall makes a superb lunch-stop. The best one-way direction to explore the Pass is from the south; out-and-back it is best from the north.

The tea-house

Coulin Pass 2

The environs of Achnashellach Station

Coulin Pass

X

Station House

narrow track

level crossing

station

Lair/Craig – (for Gleann Fhiodhaig)

private Achnashellach Lodge

A890

Strathcarron

X = alternative path to the tea house (and Torridon) – see O.S. map

Coulin Pass 3

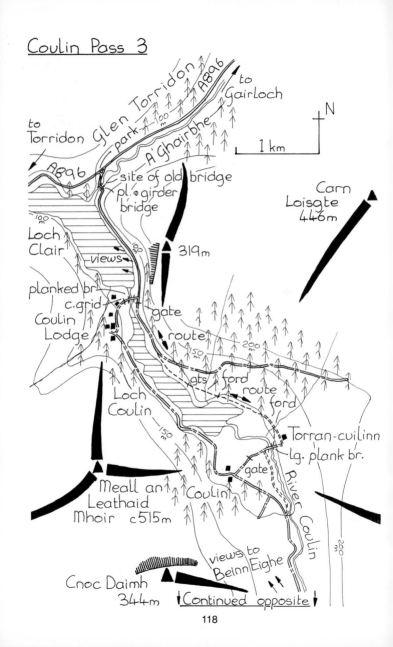

to Gairloch

1 km   N

to Torridon   A896   Glen Torridon   A896   park   100 m   A'Ghairbhe

site of old bridge
pl. girder bridge

Carn Loisgte 446m

Loch Clair   100 m   80   319m

views

planked br.
c.grid   gate
Coulin Lodge   route   200   50 m

Loch Coulin   gts   ford   route   ford   150

Torran-cuilinn   lg. plank br.

Meall an Leathaid Mhoir c515m   Coulin   gate   River Coulin   200

views to Beinn Eighe

Cnoc Daimh 344m

↑ Continued opposite ↓

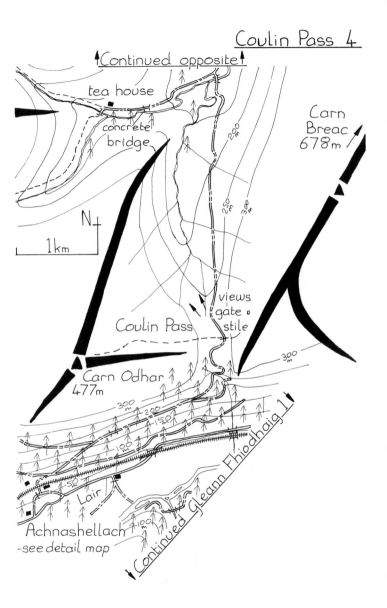

↑Continued opposite↑

tea house

concrete bridge

Carn Breac 678m ↗

N ⊥

1 km

200m

250m

300m

views
gate ○
stile

Coulin Pass

Carn Odhar
477m ↑

300m

300m

200

150

100

50

Lair

↙Continued Gleann Fhiodhaig 1

Achnashellach ↑100m↑
-see detail map

Gruinard River 1

This track leads to the site of a boathouse at the outlet of Loch na Sealga, some 8·5 km or 5·5 miles from the road around Gruinard Bay. It provides a glimpse into the Fisherfield Forest - arguably our largest area of true wilderness. The track follows all but a few hundred metres of the Gruinard River. The fact that both the boathouse and the nearby suspension bridge no longer exist strengthens the feeling of complete desolation at the end of the track; a little used path continues along the south-west side of the loch to Shenavall via a huge river crossing!

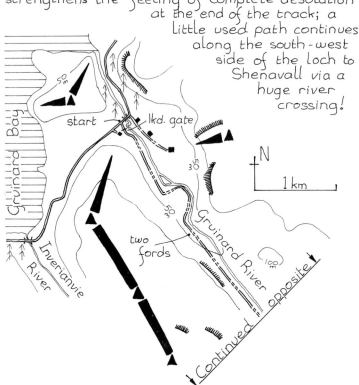

Continued opposite

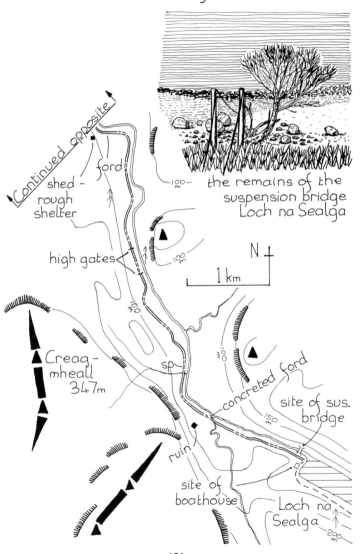

the remains of the
suspension bridge
Loch na Sealga

Continued opposite

shed -
rough
shelter

ford

100
m

high gates

N

1 km

100
m

100
m

Creag-
mheall
347m

30
m

concreted ford

150
m

site of sus.
bridge

SP

ruin

site of
boathouse

Loch na
Sealga

200
m

Gleann Chaorachain 1

The Gleann Chaorachain track provides another glimpse into the wilds of the Fisherfield Forest. Either as a return cycle ride to Achneigie, over a considerable climb, or as a walk visiting Achneigie and Shenavall returning over an often boggy path, the effort is well rewarded. The round trip via Achneigie and Shenavall is 19km or 12 miles. Achneigie is the halfway point. There is shelter only at Shenavall.

to Dundonnell

A832

50

locked gate

pk.

100
150

200
m

Glas Mheall Laith 960m

plank bridge

300

350
m

large ford

400
m

Continued

350
m

opposite

N

1 km

122

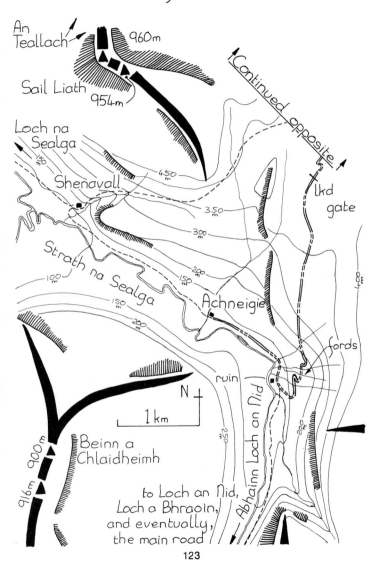

An Teallach
960m
Sail Liath
954m
Loch na Sealga
150m
Shenavall
450m
350m
300m
lkd gate
Continued opposite
Strath na Sealga
100m
150m
200m
150m
200m
Achneigie
fords
400m
ruin
N
1 km
Beinn a Chlaidheimh
900m
916m
250m
200m
Abhainn Loch an Nid
to Loch an Nid,
Loch a Bhraoin,
and eventually,
the main road

Glen Achall 1

The first mile or so of Glen Achall is spoilt by quarrying; indeed the track serves as the quarry road so beware of traffic. The start, thankfully, belies the remainder of the glen which is not only a gem, but as Link Route 1 describes, leads to a network of off-road glen tracks connecting west coast to east. The watershed is just above the south western end of Loch an Daimh but my "Glen Achall" describes the route through to Duag Bridge. Note the ford two km. west of Duag Br., and the alternative walkers' path over to Strath Mulzie. There is shelter near East Rhidorroch Lodge, at Knockdamph bothy, and beyond the ford, at Duag Bridge. However in wet weather the ford may be impassable - walkers may then cut over to Strath Mulzie. Your author met several friendly horses and three very friendly pigs who tried to eat the bike tyres!

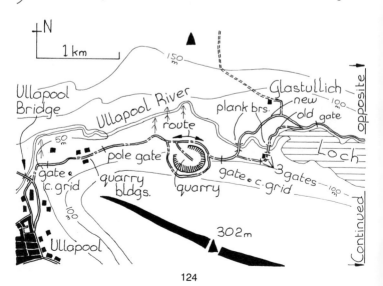

Distances are given below from the centre of Ullapool - the track starts 1km from "downtown" Ullapool but there is nowhere to park here.

One way distance to:-

	km	miles
East Rhidorroch Lodge	13	8
Knockdamph bothy	19	12
Abhainn Poiblidh ford	23	14.5
Duag Bridge (via ford)	25.5	16
[Duag Br.(via Strath Mulzie)	27.5	17]
Oykel Bridge (main road)	32.5	20
Croick (via Strath Cuileannach)	40.5	25
Strath Rusdale (end of public road - via Croick • Glen Calvie	63.5	39.5
Alness (as above + public roads)	78	48
Black Bridge (via S.Cuileannach, Gleann Mor, Strath Vaich)	71.5	44 [1]
Inchbae Lodge (as above but via Strath Rannoch)	77.5	48 [2]
Return to Ullapool by main road, add: [1]	38.5	24
[2]	41.5	26

Meall Liath Choire 548m

Achall 2

cattle grid

Cadubh

Creag Ghrianach

Loch an Eilean

300

Continued Glen

Rhidorroch River

280

100

250

150

150

200

gates

shelter

2 sm. fords

300

gate

East Rhidorroch Lodge

sm. ford

Continued opposite

N

1 km

Meall na Moch-eirigh

365m

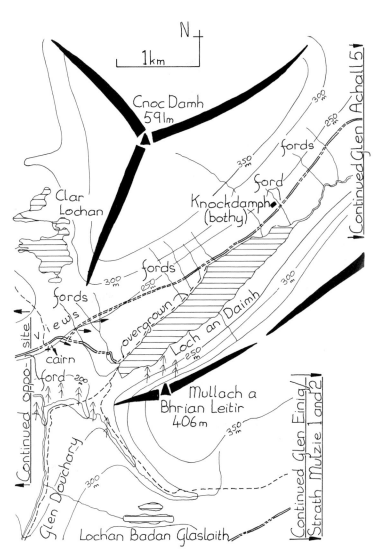

N

1km

Cnoc Damh
591m

Continued Glen Achall 5

300m

250m

fords

350m

ford

Clar
Lochan

Knockdamph
(bothy)

fords

300m

fords

250m

300m

overgrown

Loch an Daimh

views

250m

site

cairn

ford 200

Mullach a
Bhrian Leitir
406m

350m

Continued oppo-

Continued Glen Einig/
Strath Mulzie 1 and 2

Glen Douchary

300m

Lochan Badan Glaslaith

Glen Achall 5

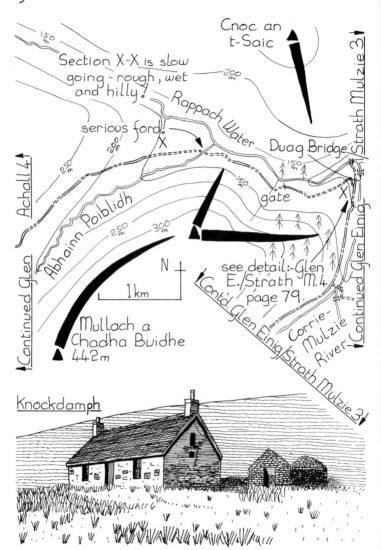

Cnoc an t-Saic

Section X-X is slow going - rough, wet and hilly!

Rappach Water

Duag Bridge

serious ford!

X

Strath Mulzie 3

Achall 4

Abhainn Poiblidh

gate

150 m

200 m

250 m

300 m

Continued Glen

N

1 km

Mullach a Chadha Buidhe 442m

see detail:- Glen E./Strath M.4 page 79.

Cont'd Glen Einig/Strath Mulzie 3

Corrie-Mulzie River

Continued Glen Einig

Knockdamph

128

The Loch Fannich 'track' is metalled for much of the way and as such makes for both tedious walking or a rapid approach to the hills by bike. The deteriorating track is **ride**able almost to the head of the Loch. From this point a walkers' path climbs to a bealach at 560m and descends to Loch a Bhraoin and the main road 6km/4m south west of Braemore Junction. (*Note:-* if descending by this path be sure to cross the burn *before* it gets too big!). There is a tenuous connection to the Lochrosque Forest track, but see the note on page 137 regarding the gate on to the main road at the start, so a circuit of Loch Fannich is possible.

Loch Fannich 2

Fannich Lodge is some 12km or 8miles from the start, and the ruin near the head of the Loch is a further 7km or 4·5 miles. The loop around the head of Loch Fannich and to the road/gate at the start of Lochrosque Forest track is 35km or 22miles. The distance back to the start of the Loch Fannich track (ie. road connection to road connection) is 12·5km or 8miles.

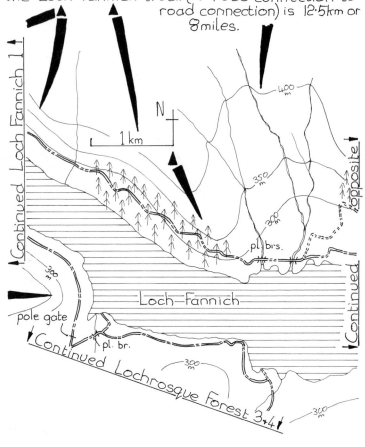

N

1 km

Continued Loch Fannich 1

Opposite

Continued

Loch Fannich

400 m

350 m

300 m

300 m

300 m

300 m

pl. brs.

pole gate

pl. br.

Continued Lochrosque Forest 3+4

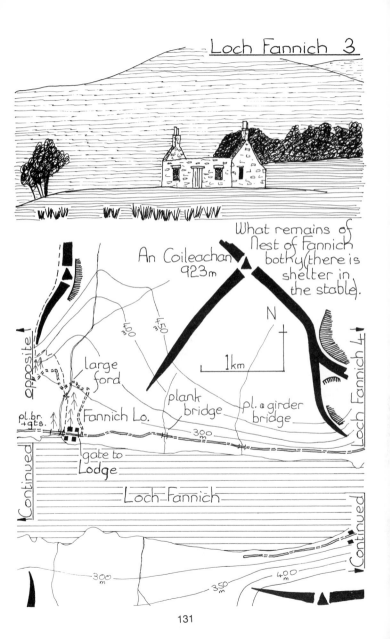

What remains of
Nest of Fannich
bothy (there is
shelter in
the stable).

An Coileachan
923 m

N

1 km

400 m

450 m

large
ford

plank
bridge

pl. @ girder
bridge

300 m

Fannich Lo.

pl. br.
+ gts.

gate to
Lodge

Loch Fannich

300 m

350 m

400 m

opposite ↑

Continued

Loch Fannich 4

Continued

Loch Fannich 4

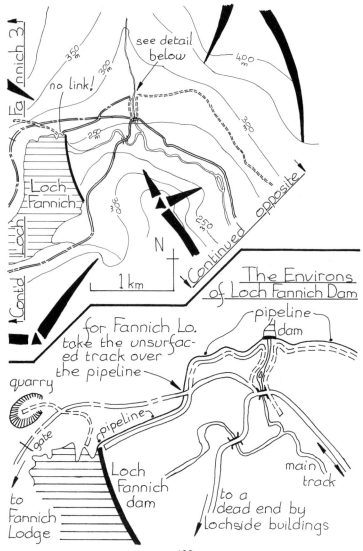

see detail below

no link!

350 m

300 m

400 m

300 m

Fannich 3

Fa

Loch Fannich

Loch Contd

250 m

300 m

250 m

N

Continued opposite

1 km

The Environs of Loch Fannich Dam

pipeline

dam

for Fannich Lo. take the unsurfaced track over the pipeline

quarry

gate

pipeline

Loch Fannich dam

to Fannich Lodge

main track

to a dead end by lochside buildings

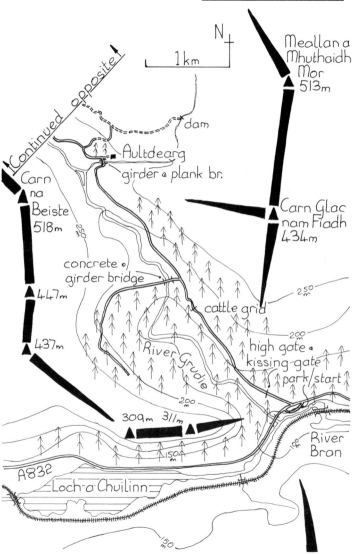

N

1 km

Meallan a
Mhuthaidh
Mor
513m

dam

Aultdearg
girder ₀ plank br.

Continued opposite

Carn
na
Beiste
518m

350
300

concrete ₀
girder bridge

447m

437m

Carn Glac
nam Fiadh
434m

250
m

cattle grid

200
m

high gate ₀
kissing gate
park/start

River Grudie

200

309m 311m

150
m

150

A832

Loch-a-Chuilinn

River
Bran

100

Lochrosque Forest 1

The Lochrosque Forest track used to lead to Cabuie Lodge, however the dam raised the loch, cutting off access to the lodge, but extending it to serve the pipeline. It ends in Strath Chrombuill - above the Heights of Kinlochewe. An even more recent track runs to the head of Loch Fannich and (just) beyond; see "Loch Fannich 1" for its continuation. Observant individuals will spot the old cast iron milepost, below, beside the track. The start is barred by a high locked gate, and fence, with unfortunately no stile - a rather unfair obstacle. The track quickly climbs to reveal Loch Fannich and explore some extremely wild country. The distance to the adit/dam above Strath Chrombuill is 15km or 9.5 miles; to the head of Loch Fannich is about the same, the junction being 9km or 5.5 miles from the start. There is no shelter other than a miserable concrete hut.

N

1 km

Just off this map but on the wrong side of the river is the Leckie track - above Heights of kinlochewe

400 m

300 m

250 m

150 m

200 m

old path

Cont'd Lochrosque Forest 3

Strath Chrombuill

250 m

views

gates   pl. brs.

300 m

400 m

300 m

ford

practical limit with a bike

dam

350 m

vague path

400 m

450 m

450

500m

Coire Bog (must be wet!)

400 300

this path eventually leads back to the main road but is now seldom used.

Lochrosque Forest 3

↑Cont'd Loch Fannich 1 & 2↑

Loch.F.

↑ Continued Lochrosque Forest 2 ↑

↑ Continued opposite ↑

400 m   450 m   lkd. pole gate

pl. br.

300 m   350 m   vague old path

pipeline   300

Strath

Chrombuill   250 m

pl. br.

gate • dam   300 m

concrete hut (open shelter)

400 m

plank bridges • adits   350 m

Loch na Moine Mor   300

450 m

N   1 km

stalkers' path

933m
Fionn Bheinn

Note:-
The head of Loch Fannich is now devoid of
civilised shelter. Cabuie Lodge was demolished
before the dam was built, but the loch never
reached the site of the lodge as expected .....
(oops!!). Nest of Fannich bothy, once a haven
in a wild and remote glen, was destroyed by
fire and is now ruinous, see sketch page 131.
All that now remains is the rubbish-strewn
stable next to the ruined bothy - but how
long will even this rough shelter remain intact?

The start

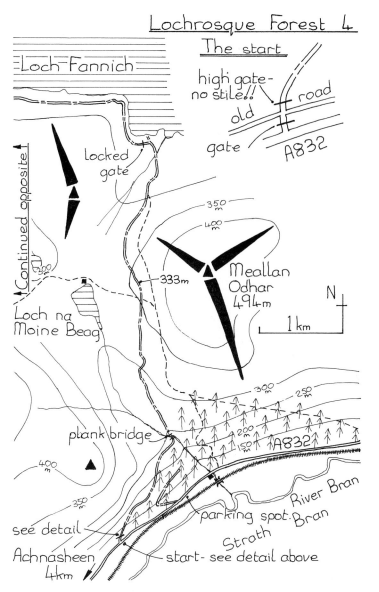

Loch Fannich

high gate - no stile!!

old road

gate

A832

Continued opposite

locked gate

350 m

400 m

333m

Meallan Odhar 494m

N

1 km

Loch na Moine Beag

300 m

250 m

200 m

150 m

A832

plank bridge

400 m

350 m

River Bran

parking spot

Strath Bran

see detail

Achnasheen 4km

start- see detail above

137

Link Routes

The link routes shown demonstrate how long through routes are made up from the various page maps. Variations can be planned using further adjacent routes but these should provide a basis for extended exploration.

The Northern Glens   ## Link Route 1

These northern glens form a unique network of linked tracks providing several options for off-road coast-to-coast cycling

or long distance walking. The only snag is the return to the starting point, though Ullapool, Black Br./Inchbae Lodge all have bus services - as does Bonar Bridge - just down the glen from Croick.

Much care is required in planning long distance cycle rides or walks in this region. Accommodation is limited to bothies or preferably your tent. Use the route either as a loop between Alness and Black Bridge/ Inchbae Lodge or, via Croick, to Strath Oykel and on to Ullapool.

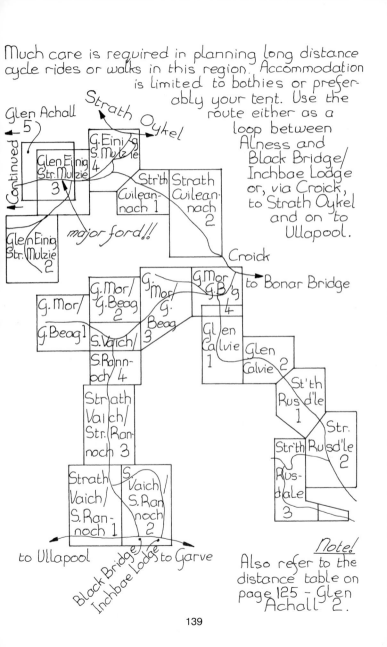

Glen Achall

Strath Oykel

← 5

Continued →

G. Eini /g
S. Mulzie 4

Glen Einig
Str. Mulzie
3

Str'th Cuileannach 1

Strath Cuileannach 2

Glen Einig
Str. Mulzie
2

major ford!!

Croick

to Bonar Bridge

G. Mor/
G. Beag
2

G. Mor/
G. Beag 1

G. Mor/
G. Beag
3

G. Mor
G. B /g
4

S. Vaich/
S. Rannoch 4

Glen Calvie
1

Glen Calvie 2

St'th Rus'd'le 1

Str. Rus'd'le 2

Strath Vaich/
Str. Rannoch 3

Str'th Rusdale 3

Strath Vaich/
S. Rannoch 1

S. Vaich/
S. Rannoch 2

to Ullapool

Black Bridge/ Inchbae Lodge

to Garve

Note!
Also refer to the distance table on page 125 – Glen Achall 2.

139

Link Route 2

Glen Moriston to Morvich

This route is best done from east to west if cycling to negotiate the rough section from Camban to Glen-Licht House downhill. A superb cross-country route with an SYHA hostel at Alltbeithe, and off-route at Cannich. No major fords, just a long demanding through route — the very best of our wild country.

Note:- Distances below are approximate due to the variety of routes between Affric and Tomich. The track to Cluanie is not a bike ride.

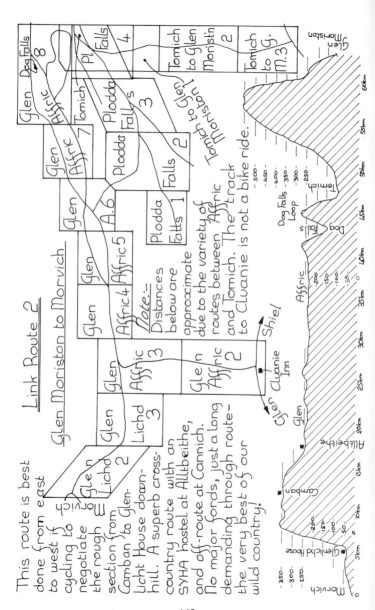

Glen Licht 2 — Glen Licht 3 — Glen — Glen Affric 3 — Glen Affric 2

Glen Affric 4 — Affric 5 — Glen A.6 — Glen Affric 7 — Tomich — Plodda Falls — Glen Affric 8

Glen Dog Falls 8 — Pl Falls 4

Plodda Falls 1 — Plodda Falls 2 — Plodda Falls 3

Tomich to Glen Moriston 1 — Tomich to Glen Moristn 2 — Tomich to G. m.3

Glen Cluanie Inn — Glen Shiel

Morvich · Glenlicht House · Camban · Alltbeithe · Affric · Dog Falls · Dog Falls Loop · Tomich · Glen Moriston

0 · 5km · 10km · 15km · 20km · 25km · 30km · 35km · 40km · 45km · 50km · 55km · 60km

140

Lochrosque Forest and Loch Fannich

This combination of two routes almost circumnavigates Loch Fannich. Off-road distance is 35km/22m with 12km/8m of road to complete the circuit.

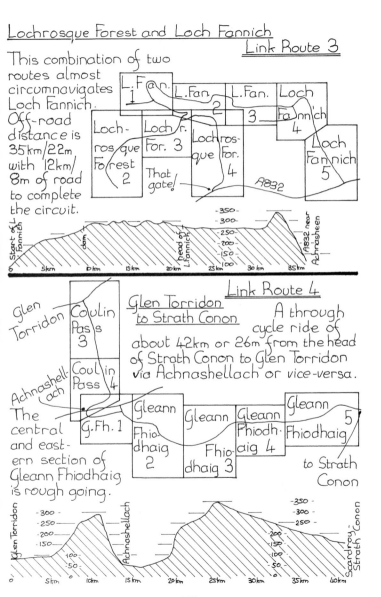

L. Fan. 1

L. Fan. 2

L. Fan. 3

Loch Fannich 4

Lochrosque Forest 2

Loch r. For. 3

Lochrosque For. 4

Loch Fannich 5

That gate!

A832

Start of L. Fannich

dam

head of L. Fannich

A832 near Achnasheen

-350-
-300-
-250-
-200-
-150-
-100

0   5km   10km   15km   20km   25km   30km   35km

Link Route 4

Glen Torridon to Strath Conon

A through cycle ride of about 42km or 26m from the head of Strath Conon to Glen Torridon via Achnashellach or vice-versa.

The central and eastern section of Gleann Fhiodhaig is rough going.

Glen Torridon

Coulin Pass 3

Achnashellach

Coulin Pass 4

G.Fh. 1

Gleann Fhiodhaig 2

Gleann Fhiodhaig 3

Gleann Phiodhaig 4

Gleann Fhiodhaig 5

to Strath Conon

Glen Torridon

Achnashellach

Scardroy - Strath Conon

-300-
-250-
-200-
-150-
-100-
-50

-350-
-300-
-250-
-200-
-150-
-100-
-50

0   5km   10km   15km   20km   25km   30km   35km   40km

141

Well, that's it folks! Nine books and the series is complete. Anti-climax? Yes. Relief? Yes, at having stayed the course and not given up on what grew into an enormous task - a labour of love - but nevertheless my wife and I had to stick to the job in hand. Over the ten years or so we have enjoyed some 350 days in our wild places, spent around 50 days getting to and fro, and yours truly has written, sketched and drawn 1200 pages over 400 days. We have worn out two complete bikes, four pairs of wheels, eight pairs of tyres, two bums, smashed a dictation machine, yet only had one puncture (and yes, it was raining at the time!). My wife and I have each ridden over 7500 miles off-road (12,000 km sounds more impressive!) and walked a few hundred miles.... and all that's research - we walk, mountainbike and cycle for fun as well!

So, where are the best places to go off-road in the Highlands? My own choice of best centre, best glen/route and best link route book by book is as follows:-

Book 1 The Cairngorm Glens :- best centre, Braemar; best glen, Glen Avon; best link route, The Cairngorm Circuit.

Book 2 The Atholl Glens :- best centre, Blair Atholl; best glen, Glen Tilt; best link route, Glen Tilt/Glen Fearnach.(or Tilt/Feshie - Book 1)

Book 3 The Glens of Rannoch:- best centres, Fort William or Loch Rannoch(near-not in!); best glen, Strath Ossian; best link route, Dalwhinnie to Fort William.

Book 4 The Trossach Glens :- best centre, Callander; best glen, Glen Almond; best link route, Loch Ard to Loch Tay.

Book 5 The Glens of Argyll:- best centre, Ardgartan; best glen, Glen Kinglass(Etive); best link route, Circuit of Ben Cruachan.

Book 6 The Great Glen:- best centre, Fort Augustus; best glen, River Dulnain ; best link route, Dava to Rothes (or the Great Glen Cycle Route).

Book 7 The Angus Glens:- best centres, Ballater or Banchory; best glen, Glen Muick; best link route, the West Angus Glens (walking).

Book 8 Knoydart to Morvern:- best centres, Fort William or Ratagan (Shiel Bridge); best glen, Glen Kingie or Loch Garry; best link route, The South Glenshiel Circuit.

Book 9 The Glens of Ross-shire:- best centre, Cannich; best glen, Glen Affric; best link route, The Northern Glens - Alness to Ullapool.

The best places are, of course, those isolated glens, bathed in sunshine, with no pressure of time, reached through our own efforts no matter whether by bike or on foot, in the company of our choosing (or alone!)... Any of the suggested routes can provide, on the right day, all of this; it is there for the taking, free, wild and uncomplicated......

Incidentally, we have only once been ticked off by the-bloke-in-the-Land-Rover whose misguided interpretation of "access" differentiated between cyclists and pedestrians. "Bike or boots - what matter ?" They" will ban walking sticks next! Good manners always helps.

To sum up I must thank my publisher for his support in the task of producing and marketing these guides, and you, dear reader, for buying them! Thanks also to my wife for her untiring (except after a long day on the bike!) support, company and practical help (like feeding me). Hopefully, all this has resulted in many thousands of days out enjoying our wild places; if so, then your author is satisfied indeed with the completion of his self-imposed task.